From Sick *to* Bliss *to* Conversations with God

From Sick *to* Bliss *to* Conversations with God

ANGELA MIA WHITE

Blissful Flow

Dedication

THIS BOOK IS DEDICATED to many, many people, but first and foremost to the God of my soul. I am humbled to be a part of Your plan and grateful that You are using me and my family's life as a powerful conduit, healing tool, and vehicle for people to awaken to what really is. Love is what we are. As you read this book you will start to understand that statement. I am so grateful to know and correspond with Mother Mary, Jesus, the Angels, Ascended Masters, Saints, and the Ancestors of love and light. All thanks goes to them all as they have had a huge part in this. Thank you for the assistance in writing this book. It gives me much comfort that you all know my soul. I love you all.

This book has a special dedication to my exceptional husband Gary. For being the person you are and the way you show your unwavering, undying love for me and our boys. For your dedication to me as I was sick and as I was healing; and going through all of these changes speaks volumes about who you are. The love you put into our family every day to make it what it is, is beyond what I ever expected in a husband. I couldn't have stayed alive nor done any of this without you. I will always remember what you have done for me. It is an honor and privilege to know you, be by your side as your wife, and join you on your own journey of awakening. Remember that you are worth it, always have been worth it, and always will be worth it. Always and forever, my love.

To our three beautiful boys Zachary, Anthony and Cody, I am and will forever be grateful to you for helping me to get to this point in my life. Thank you for all you did to help me walk, talk, and love again; I am in your debt. Thank you for believing in me even when I didn't believe in myself. You gave me reason to keep fighting to live. I love you with every ounce of my being. This journey of life will be different for each of you. You can find out what you are meant to do by going inside and knowing and loving yourself. There is energy there that shifts the Earth! All the answers for you, are inside of you and only you, for you. Find the spark of the Divine that you are. You each have a specific purpose in this life. Believe in yourself, love yourself, and live your purpose. We will change this Planet together. All of my love goes to each of you, always.

To all these beautiful people: my mom, my dad, Joey, Donna, my sisters, brothers, all of my sweet friends who waited, watched, helped, prayed, sent cards, texted, emailed, wrote to me on Facebook and helped be there for my children during this time, "thank you" just seems like it will never be enough to say. I love you all and I am and will be forever grateful to you for everything.

To Dr. Robert Morse and Dr. Sarika Arora, for giving me what I needed to survive, so that this book could be written. Thank you for your love and truth.

To the people who have challenged me in my life and brought out all the ugly feelings and emotions that have been programmed into me over the years, I am sorry if I hurt you and I thank you for loving me. You have given me what I needed so that I could choose to release from within that which no longer served me. As I let go, I am able to receive more love and light. I am eternally grateful.

To Monya and Marcia: I have no idea how to thank you for bringing me through this journey, helping me discover on my own, that we are Love. There are no limits. It is absolutely freeing and has allowed me to, finally, breathe. Thank you for helping me to liberate my mind and soul and teaching me the "dance." Thank you both for the many years of walking in the path of love and light, a path on which I have now joined you, to help others be able to *see*. You hold a special place in my heart. You have helped me believe in myself and believe that I was in fact chosen to do this. You have given me courage to put my "special boots" on and walk. I love you both. Love, light, joy, and peace, my soul sisters.

To all my new friends on Facebook from around the World: thank you for being my friends and my support. Thank you for sustaining me in love and abundance as I finished this book. It is due to you, and your messages of love to me, that helped me to see that everyone needs to know what we know. I hope you know how much you are loved by me. I hope to meet you someday on this Earth plane or another dimension of time. We are one.

From Sick to Bliss to Conversations with God
Angela Mia White

F I R S T   E D I T I O N
Hardcover ISBN: 9781939288660
Library of Congress Control Number: 2014940517
eBook ISBN: 9781939288707

Blissful.Flow111

Blissful.Flow

BlissfullyAngela

Published Blissful Flow,
An Imprint of Wyatt-MacKenzie

Blissful Flow

www.blissfulflow.com

Table of Contents

Preface

I MYSELF LIKE BOOKS that are easy to read and that get to the point. This will be that type of book. I don't have the gift of gab, but I have been given many other gifts and so have you. You can find out what those gifts are once you know yourself.

I say this with the utmost love and respect for you, the reader, as you deserve both. I am not writing this book to try to convince you of anything, nor am I writing it to seek fame or fortune. I have been directed to write this book. I didn't even choose the title; it was given to me. I was even told how it was going to get published and paid for. I have also been instructed to illustrate the unity of the Planet, Earth, World, and Universe by writing them as proper nouns. I never in a million years thought that I would write a book, let alone be able to publish it. It has basically written itself. I have been the one behind the keyboard, but the reason this book has been written is much bigger than I. It has been written for a specific purpose. It is to wake you up to *you*. This is for all the people who feel stuck, who do not feel free, who do not feel worthy, who do not understand themselves and think that it is wrong to love themselves. I am the example that the Angels are using to show you just how important it is to know and love yourselves. Not your ego, but your spirit. The ego is what we all hide behind every day to walk in this life, because we are too afraid to be who we really are, which is love. They want us to know it is okay to be who we are in our soul. In fact they need us to do that. Doing so will help shift the consciousness of the Planet that much faster. We are ushering in an age of "peace." This is a very special time on this Planet; I have been chosen to write about and to invite you to learn, if you choose, how to partake in it.

I, along with my family, have lived this metamorphosis for two years. I take full responsibility for all of it: the past, present, and what is to come from this. I am not claiming to have "all the answers." I am not trying to change your thinking of the Bible, your thoughts about it, your religion, or lack thereof. That is your journey. You must decide for yourself what you believe and what no longer serves you. You need to take responsibility for yourself. I am just sharing what I have gone through and am continuing to go through. These are the things that I have been taught, have experienced, witnessed, and have been told. I have quoted passages from the Bible that portray the essence of who I see Jesus to be, as well as some scripture stories that some scholars question if we should take literally. During this journey my mother told me that there was a book called *The Messengers* by Julia Ingram and G. W. Hardin. It is about a man named Nick Bunick; it is about his life today and his life as Paul the apostle in another lifetime. He walked with Jesus. My mother bought this book back in the 1990s. She just took it off her bookshelf recently and told me that I needed to read it, as this book told the same things that I had been telling her I have been "told" by my Angels. The stories told in the book about Nick Bunick's life are different from mine, but what we have in common is that we were both directed by the Angels to write our books. Nick and I are on the same conscious plane with them, and I wouldn't want to be anywhere else.

Healing is a process that we all must go through. You may not have a physical healing to do; it may still just be emotional healing, but I can guarantee that you need to heal from some type of hurt in your life. It is a process, and on the other side of it, if you choose, there can be a beautiful, loving, and miraculous awakening. You may choose to believe it or not. It is all up to you. You are on your own path in life and so am I. I found Me and You can find You.

The sole purpose and intent of this book is to help people with their own healing and awakening. Freely I have received, and freely I give. This is who my God is and who I *am*.

In the Beginning

THIS STORY IS SIMPLY about my life and how I went from sickness to bliss to conversations with God and many things in between. This healing of my body came about without the aid of prescription medication, radiation, chemotherapy, or over-the-counter drugs. With that being said, please do not do anything without talking to your doctors. This story is not meant to diagnose or take the place of a doctor's orders. It is also not intended to dismiss these procedures that may be necessary in some circumstances.

I went from being a pretty happy mom and wife, so I thought, to not being able to walk, not being able to talk or think straight, to now communicating with the spiritual World. I am also becoming a medium; as my life progresses more and more, gifts are being birthed, such as channeling Angels, Mother Mary, and now conversations with God. I know it sounds impossible in this physical World, but it is really taking place in my life.

I hope this story of my journey of the last two years will help you see how our bodies are capable of healing with love and intent. On this physical plane, the body, mind, and spirit are seen as separate. In my experience as I awaken to what is, I see spiritually that they are one; it's a flow. As you awaken you will be able to see your soul. The soul in you is the spark of the Divine, God, Source, Yahweh, Jesus, Buddha, or whatever you were brought up to call this entity. To me it is all the same. I was brought up to call Him God; in essence, Love. If you call this Source something else, please insert that where God is used. If you are sick right now, please take a deep breath and start reading how my body healed itself. Your body is designed that way, too. If you are not sick and just on a journey of awakening, please read on; I think this may help. I wish you much health, happiness and most of all love—Namaste*

—Angela Mia

---

* Which means "The divine light in me honors the divine light in you," or "The God within me greets the God within you."

How it all started

Slowing Down

IT WAS A BEAUTIFUL SUNNY DAY on June 10, 2012. It was my younger sister Val's birthday and a combined graduation party of both of our children. My oldest, Zachary, and her second oldest, Lyndsi. The sun was beginning to set and we had just started to clean up the remains of the celebration. Things seemed fine with me while setting up the party and during it. It was hectic and fun as all parties usually are. I didn't notice that things in my system were a bit off. I was not listening to my body. I really just tried to ignore the signals as much as I could and get through the party.

As I was starting the cleanup, I noticed something odd. My body started slowing down. It started with just feeling the pull of gravity on my body. It felt like every movement I made was harder than the last. Every dish I picked up and tried to put away felt as though it weighed a ton. I thought I was just tired.

I remember talking to Donna in the kitchen and we were just discussing how successful the party had been, and we were talking about my son Zac and where he was going to attend college. As I was talking, I noticed that the words that I was trying to say were coming out of my mouth a lot more slowly than I wanted them to. I tried to keep up with the conversation without thinking too much about what was happening.

From what I remember I woke up the next morning and felt pretty good. I was still slow though. I thought maybe I was just coming down with something.

Lesson of Worrying Before Getting Sick

Our lives were a bit hectic before I started getting sick. We, my husband Gary and I, own and manage property. This includes renting, fixing the property, paying the bills, taking care of emergencies etc. A few months before this we had three fires; yes, three of our buildings had fires. Many people go through life without one fire. We had three in about three months' time. No one was hurt in any of them, thank God. One of the fires was a total loss. The whole apartment complex of 32 apartments was destroyed. We owned only one of those 32, but the loss was still devastating and time consuming. In the second fire, the building had excessive water damage so severe that all three floors of 21 units and a manager apartment needed to be completely ripped out and had to be redone. The third fire was not as bad as either of the first two, but it just added stress to everything else.

I have always been a huge worrier. I had no idea that it was pulling events into my life that I didn't want to happen. The Universe always says, yes. When you worry, you pull whatever you are worrying about into your existence. The Universe is always giving us situations in our lives that will allow us to get in touch with feelings that no longer serve us, name those feelings, identify where in our lives we have felt this way before, and then deal with them and release them.

For example, before I got sick in April of 2012, we went on a family vacation to Florida. My husband, our three boys, and two of their friends all traveled in one Tahoe. While in Florida, my oldest son Zachary, at age 18, wanted to take our vehicle to drive to Parris Island, South Carolina with his friend Alberto, to watch their friend Billy graduate from Marine boot camp. I was pretty much against this as he was still a new driver. He assured me that nothing was going to happen and that they would be fine. He and his friend took the Tahoe and made it to South Carolina. On the way home there was a fierce rainstorm. There was a phone call to my husband and I just looked at him and I said, "Are they okay"? He said, "Yes, but the Tahoe is pretty damaged". I thanked God they were okay. It was a chain reaction so they were hit from the back into the car in front of them. We went home with a damaged Tahoe and some shaken up kids, but lesson learned.

> *"Worrying is praying for something that you don't want*
> *to happen. So stop worrying."*
> *– Bhagavan Das*

People Are People

As I said, we are landlords and good ones at that. Owning and renting your own apartments have some positive and negative aspects to them. One of the negative aspects to being landlords is that your friends, at times, need places to live. We have had many friends ask us to rent to them. Gary and I are givers; we always have been and always will be. We try to help anyone we encounter. Gary is a caretaker by nature. Everyone knows that if something happens, Gary will be there to help, if they ask. So, when our friends were in need of places to live, it was only natural that we wanted to help them. There are always people who will take advantage of you. This happens many times, but when it is your friends, people you love and trust, it makes it that much worse. This has also happened to us more than a few times. I took all the times that this happened to us to heart and wouldn't let it go. It was a personal attack against Gary and me. We are good people and didn't deserve this. This is how I *used* to feel. Now, I understand that people are people and they are just doing what they know how to do, and a lot of decisions are made from fear. I have learned that when you hold onto negative things, they fester. It just gets worse and worse. You don't want to hold onto anything negative. Let it go!

What Are We Going to Teach Our Children About God?

Zachary Is Born

WHEN MY HUSBAND AND I were little, we were baptized as babies and raised Catholic. Our parents were Catholic so they naturally raised us as such. Both of our parents got divorced and Gary and I always said that we would always try to work out our problems. The beginning of our marriage was kind of rough. We didn't think the problems would arrive so quickly, but they did. We went to counseling and wanted to stay together. We agreed to try to make it work. We had our problems, like everyone else. We did get through this difficult time in our marriage, but it was a lot of work to try to stay together. I didn't know this back then, but what I know now is that your life is about you. You must work on yourself for things to get better in your life; what you see and take out on others is a direct reflection of what you are feeling about, you.

Zachary was born in July of 1994, three and a half years into our marriage. He was everything to us. He started us on our quest of "What are we going to teach him about God?" We had stopped going to church long before that, but because of Zachary we started going to the Catholic Church again. When I went to church, things began changing for me. I no longer saw Jesus on the cross as just a statue. He started becoming real to both of us. Both Gary and I started a journey together and we started to see God in our lives. In the summer of 1995 we started meeting people who had our same interests at heart and it eventually led us to people from a nondenominational Christian church. In the early fall of 1995, Gary and I studied the Bible. We were baptized into this church. This was where our hearts led us, so this is where we were supposed to be for a time. We were very much involved and a part of the church. We would go to church every chance we got. We had Bible talks, and church services on Sundays and Wednesdays. It was our life. We became Bible-talk leaders while we were still very new in the church and really did not know what we were doing; but we had the hearts to learn and help people. So, that is what we did.

We were in that church until our youngest son Cody was born in 2001. During those years we met a lot of wonderful people. It was very family oriented, but it was also a type of a confining existence, as everyone had accountability for everyone else; it was all scripture based, and there was not much flow (recently, in one of my conversations with God, He said He is "flow."). I will let you know about this later. We were all for it, though. It was helping our marriage and helping us to be a happy family. We had made wonderful friends in the church who cared about us and our spiritual well-being. Who wouldn't want that? But something still felt pretty confining. I am realizing now that God is not confining. Your soul will die if confined. It wants to be free. God does not want to be put into a box. Something else that I am realizing is that we can only do the best we can from where we are in life and with what information we have at the time. Most everyone is trying their best. Don't beat yourself up for a decision you made ten years ago that you probably wouldn't make today. It was there for a reason to get you where you are today. We are all learning. Give yourself grace.

Anthony Is Born

During our years in this church, in June of 1996, our second son, Anthony was born. After I had Anthony, I realized that something wasn't right. I had "postpartum depression," but I did not understand what it was. I remember that I would sit in my living room and it seemed all of the living room furniture got smaller and smaller until I would eventually have a panic attack. It was a very scary and strange feeling. I felt as if I was leaving my body. I had no idea what this was at the time. I understand now that it was, in fact, me leaving my body because I didn't want to be in it. As we were in the church then, getting advice was commonplace: that is what we were taught to do. We were to get advice on pretty much everything; did that mean we should not make decisions on our own? I was told, by my Bible-talk leader at that time, that "I shouldn't diagnose myself and that it probably wasn't happening."

So I suffered in silence for a while just pretending that it wasn't happening and trying to cover it up with scriptures and prayer. At the time, I had put my faith in all these people because this is where God was to me. I did end up getting some psychiatric help and they put me on depression medication to get through. I had no idea why I was going through what I was going through, but I knew that what I was feeling was not normal. I blame no one. It was a journey that I needed to be on to discover the rest of my life. This is simply what these Bible-talk leaders are taught to do. It was what I was taught to do. I understand that now. I think for myself now and take responsibility for my life and the decisions I make.

Cody Was Born and I Realized That I Am an Empath

It was 2001 and I was pregnant a third time with our son Cody. Cody was born late December 2001. This was a few months after 9/11 happened. I felt extremely guilty that I had two beautiful boys, a wonderful husband, was alive with a baby on the way and these people perished a horrible death. I took that all in, also. Feelings were always incredibly intense to me; so much so that I would feel physical pain from it. I am an Empath. An Empath is a person who takes on other people's energies, good or bad. I never knew such a thing existed. I always thought that I was just extremely sensitive and needed to just deal with it. Please believe me, if you are feeling things intensely like this, you do not have to suffer from it. If you are highly sensitive to feeling the emotions of others, you are probably some type of Empath. Being an Empath without realizing it can be detrimental to your health. If you do not know how to protect yourself against the feelings of others, you will take those feelings onto yourself. First, it is very unhealthy to take on other people's feelings and emotions; second, it is not your emotion. It is not fair to you and not fair to them to take the emotions that are someone else's; you need to let people live their own lives. They deserve it and so do you. If you need help with this, there are many articles and websites that can help you to deal with being an Empath. Just knowing that this is actually true, helped me.

My Hell on Earth

After giving birth to Cody in 2001, I was very sick again with "postpartum depression." It was a kind of psychotic depression. It was so very bad that Gary couldn't leave me alone for too long with our children. This was extremely humbling and depressing. I was very depressed; I didn't want anyone around me, I couldn't talk on the phone, I couldn't answer the door. I was trying to hide from the World and from myself. I did not realize how much emotion I was carrying around with me. I was having major panic attacks and really didn't go out of the house unless I was forced to do so.

At that time, I went to see a psychiatrist who works with women suffering from post-partum psychosis. She was a lovely soul and understood what I was going through. I was prescribed several different medications. I was on all kinds of anti-depressant and anti-anxiety medications. The dosages needed to be increased week after week until I was at a very high dosage on all of these medications. These medications were the only treatment I was aware of that could possibly keep me somewhat sane. As the months went on, I was probably up to about 14 pills a day. It was my hell on Earth. During this time, my friend came over with scriptures and tried to encourage me with them. The most prominent thing I remember was that I felt like I was jumping out of my skin. It was a feeling of dread, so intense that it was nauseating at times. It was continuous and only let up for brief periods of time. I remember telling her that I just felt "raw." There was no other way to describe it. This is what I now understand to have been me leaving my body, as I didn't want to be in it. I ended up being on this medication for ten years. Over those years, I did my best to cut down the amount of medication. I tried to wean myself off of all of them, but I just couldn't wean off completely. My body felt so sick when I tried to do this. I was able to eventually reduce the number and dosages of medications, but I still needed some of this medication to function. Then I was having a hard time sleeping, so I started to add other pills to what I was taking, especially sleep medication.

After about a year, when I finally got to a level of saneness that allowed me to communicate with people, I tried going back to our church and Bible groups; when I did, I felt sick to my stomach and had panic attacks. I was trying to heal, so I just stayed away from these things; the day came that we just didn't go back at all anymore. I felt intensely guilty that I wasn't attending services or Bible group. I also didn't understand how going to the church, a place where I really wanted to be, made me feel so ill. I continued to pray and read the Bible, but not as much as I had previously done. I think now that maybe my body was trying to tell me something.

Love Is...

Loving Yourself Is a Necessity

A COUPLE YEARS AFTER Cody was born I started going to see a different psychologist. I saw her every two weeks for several years and I got to be pretty good friends with her. She helped me deal with a lot and helped me let go of some trauma and emotions that had been generated during my teenage years. She was a great help to me; but then she started having some major problems of her own and I began to counsel her when going to these sessions. One day it was so bad that I happened to bump into her in the parking lot before my appointment and she was under the influence, so I offered to drive her home in her own car. This was my last appointment with her. The Angels tell me all the time, "No judgments." I make no judgment against her. I love her and am very grateful for her help. This was a pattern with me. I would attract people who would take advantage of me. I did not realize how unloved I felt and how unloved I was—unloved not by others, but unloved by me. I did not love myself and hadn't for years. At that time, I didn't know who I was.

When I was in the Christian church, the way I interpreted things was that loving yourself was selfish and wrong and that giving was what God wanted for us. I lived like this for a long time. Not loving myself kept me very far away from dealing with anything about me. This took the focus off me and onto a God that was far away from me. I didn't realize that I was bypassing God, by bypassing myself. I now know better.

If You Can't Give Out Love, It Doesn't Come Back to You

When you are a giver and you give, there will be takers, and takers there were. I would keep giving and they would keep taking. As much as I wanted to be filled up with God so that I could give more, it seemed to me (though not anyone else) that what I was giving was never enough. I remember one of my Bible-talk leaders saying, "It is not about finding yourself, it is about God." The way I took that was that if my life was anything about me or for me, it was wrong. Why would God give us life, breath, and everything else if He didn't want our life to matter? I now know that loving yourself is a necessity. It's so important to love yourself in order for you to be able to receive the love from anyone else, especially the love from the God of the Universe. If you can't give it out, it won't come back to you; and you can't give it out, if you don't have it to give. This love comes from yourself to yourself. Some people think that loving themselves will turn them into someone who is proud and arrogant. Just the opposite happens; when you truly love yourself, your soul, you also realize how much you are truly loved by God and everything in the Universe, and it humbles you and fills you with love. Ego will go away because you won't need it. Be proud that you are the spark of the Divine, The Great I AM. This is who we all are. These things have all been given to me to share with you. I will forever be grateful for these truths, as I believe that knowing these things started to turn my sickness around.

Love Is and Will Always Be Essential

As my sickness in 2012 progressed, I was continuing to deteriorate in respect to losing mobility. I remember that in the summer of 2012, I was going to my son's baseball games and that I tried to explain what was happening to me to my friends. I tried to explain it the best I could, but since they were not going through it, it was not easy for them to understand. It was the oddest feeling, one of having a hard time moving; it wasn't because I was tired. My friends and family just watched me week by week get worse.

I remember that in the thick of this sickness, my sister Chrissy called me one day to see how I was feeling. This phone call from her was significant in that it helped me to realize that I needed love to heal. I remember saying to her, "This is one of the hardest things that I have ever been through and I need to know you love me." She said she was so sorry for what I was going through and of course she loved me. I told her I didn't know why I needed to hear it, but I did. Why did I need to know this? Why did I need to hear it? Because love is essential and it is what heals. At that point I didn't know how to love myself and my body was crying out for it. Everyone and everything needs love.

The Downward Spiral

Losing Mobility

IN LATE JUNE OF 2012, the loss of mobility continued to worsen. I was starting to limp on my left side. I also noticed that I was not shutting the refrigerator door, I forgot my children's names, I used different words for something that had nothing to do with what I was talking about. This also got worse. I started getting scared because it was not going away and things were just getting worse. I called my doctor and explained what was happening. She wanted to see me. I went in and showed her what was happening. By this time, I was limping quite a bit and my legs and arms had started tingling. I was showing her how I was walking with a limp. She wanted me to do some tests including an MRI to see if I had any lesions on my brain. The MRI came out that there were some spots but nothing like if I had MS.

It seemed as though I had a lot of the MS symptoms, but I didn't quite fit the complete description.

Some weeks went by and I saw my doctor a few more times. I took a Lyme disease test three times and a special Lyme disease test once, as far as I can remember. All tests were negative. My doctor still had nothing definitive to tell me. I was a square peg in a round hole. I knew she felt bad for me, because I could see that she truly wanted to help me; but she had no idea how to do this. Most physical sickness has an emotional component to it. You are the one who most likely knows why you are sick.

A few more weeks went by and things were progressing quite rapidly; I was starting to have heart palpitations, shortness of breath, and my blood pressure was everywhere. Standing for long periods of time was impossible, and my brain fog was worsening. I remember that at one point, I had my husband converse with my family to let them know that I could not carry on a conversation on the phone or even in a visit. If they wanted to get in touch with me they could email me, because that gave me some time to read and understand what they were saying, and understand what I was writing back to them. It was very distressing trying to be a mother, wife, daughter, friend, sister, etc., when I couldn't understand what people were saying to me. My friends and my family checked in on me, but there was nothing I could tell them that was any different or better and I could hardly speak; even when I did, it didn't make sense. So I hardly communicated with anyone. This was a dark time in my journey. I didn't know the Angels were with me the whole time.

My Body Was Shutting Down

My doctor wanted to help me. I know she did. I could see it in her face. She sent me to see a neurologist. I went to a few appointments with the neurologist and did a few tests with them and still there were no answers.

I had no idea what was happening. No one could tell me why my body was shutting down, but it was in fact shutting down. A friend of ours, Sue, is a nurse at a hospital in Boston. She told me to go to this hospital to see if they could tell me anything or do a workup on me. Surely Boston hospitals would be able to diagnose me with something. Something would be better than "I don't know." On July 4th, 2012, I woke up and could not walk at all. My husband and I went to Boston and by the time we got into the emergency room, I was not able to speak. I was in pretty bad shape. I left at the end of the day with an appointment with a prominent neurologist in Boston. Boston was surely the place where they were going to be able to tell me what was going on with me. We went to the neurologist in Boston and he had the same answer: "We don't know." They suggested that it may be from migraine headaches. I have never heard of anyone not walking because of migraine headaches. It is not the doctors' fault. They don't know. Only I knew.

Doctors Didn't Know

That was it. I was extremely frustrated with doctors. My doctor didn't know, the neurologists didn't know, the ER didn't know. All we knew at this point was that I was in fact getting worse and there was nothing we knew of at the time that we could do to help me get better. I was at the mercy of God. I prayed and asked, "Why am I so sick and no one can diagnose me with anything"? This was my question because I had been taught to believe that any illness should have a name. I am finding out that this isn't so.

At this point I could barely eat and I drank very little. I was nauseous much of the time and didn't have an appetite. I was losing weight and my walking was intermittent. I remember that my husband had to carry me up and down the stairs frequently because my body just didn't work. He is a saint, by the way.

My quest continued, trying to determine the reason that I was so sick. I was thinking to myself, "If I don't find out what the heck is wrong with me, I am going to die." I did not want to die. I have a wonderful husband, three beautiful children and I was not going to die. I started searching more ferociously on the internet, always looking for an answer to my questions. "Why am I so sick? Why can't anyone tell me what is wrong with me?" Then I found a knight in shining armor. Dr. Robert Morse from Florida. The light coming from his heart was brilliant.

The Beginning of My Healing

The Starting of "Awakening My Soul"
With Dr. Morse

IN RESEARCHING MORE and more of Dr. Morse's videos about how to heal, I was led to more information on healing. What I realized was that my search results created a type of portal. This portal was the starting point of my soul waking up. I was waking up from a life of unconscious living to the consciousness of the blessed Universe. It was knocking on my door and I was there to answer it. It has been a progressive process of one thing leading to another to bring me where I am today in communicating with a higher realm and understanding who I really am; who we all, really are. We are love.

Dr. Robert Morse has been helping people heal themselves for 30 years. He has his own herbs that he makes called "God's Herbs." This was amazing in itself that they were called God's Herbs. He had many videos on YouTube about how to help yourself heal. There was something about him that was just beautiful. He had a spirit about him that was truly aware. He knew and could tell me why I was sick. His heart is about truth and truth he told. Through these videos he told me in a nutshell what was wrong.

I watched one video from him on YouTube that put Fibromyalgia, Lyme disease and MS all together in one discussion of how to heal from these illnesses. I was intrigued that he would put these particular health issues together in the same video and how each could be resolved, so I watched and listened. Then I started watching and listening to many of his other videos. He continued to say the same thing. It was all acidosis. He said that our diets are mostly acid. When acid takes over in our bodies, we are done. We need to have a balanced pH in our bodies and alkaline foods will help us combat and balance the acids. He taught how your body heals itself and that we are energy. There was something about what he was saying that I trusted. He didn't want my money, he wanted me well; and not only me, but the whole World. He was different than anyone that I have ever encountered. He taught me to save my life and I will forever be thankful to him. He taught me how to start juicing, to cut out meat, bread, dairy and processed foods. Normally, people have time to cut these things out gradually, as a transition in diet; but in my case, I started eating only fruit, as I was not eating much of anything anyway at that time. I asked my husband to watch these videos from Dr. Morse to see what he thought. It sounded strange to him also, but we both decided that it was worth a shot as no one else could tell us anything; really, what did we have to lose? I ate watermelon for about a month. Gary would have to cut it up into little pieces and spoon feed me. I had nothing else but watermelon, water, all kinds of God's Herbs for every system in my body and Heal All Tea that Dr. Morse also makes from these precious herbs.

In late August of 2012, I made a Skype appointment with one of Dr. Morse's colleagues. His name was Roger. I gave Roger a list of my symptoms and he explained the standard American diet: "SAD" for short. This diet that we are all most likely eating, stops your lymph system from working properly. One of Dr. Morse's statements on his videos is "Move that lymph!!" The way I understand it is that we have lymph nodes all over our body, including our tonsils and appendix. These are our wastebaskets, if you will, for our bodies; these wastebaskets need to get emptied or they overflow and disease prevails. Most people are not taught this, unless you were brought up in a setting of utilizing all natural products and foods. That isn't all that Dr. Morse talked about. He also talked about out-of-body experiences, astral travel, and spirits that enjoy hanging around our negative energy and more things that I had no idea about. I found it intriguing that he would talk about such things on a health video. But again, he was a good soul. I listened and watched more of his videos. I was still questioning things about my diet, as it wasn't that bad. Could it be something else? I started to think that maybe it's not just a physical sickness. I thought that maybe there was more to this than what I was aware of.

Starting Juicing

It was still August 2012, and I knew that the first thing that I needed to do was stop taking all my medications. Under the supervision of my psychiatrist who prescribed the medicine, I slowly started weaning myself off all the medications. It took about a month to stop everything. This was the same month as I was eating just watermelon. I was finally free of these chemical substances and it felt great!

I bought an Omega juicer and I started to juice, to live. Once you start the juicing process, detox can be strong. The detox process that I went through was not pretty. It can be a very challenging time to get through. I looked at it as though I had no choice. I was backed into a corner and needed to do this for me and for my family. I remember that I started to get a rash. It started on my side and progressed until it was everywhere on my body. This rash was red and bumpy; it stung in places and was very itchy and the itching did not stop at night. I stayed awake scratching all night at times. I remember the first rash lasted for about 12 days. The second time I got the rash I was eating nothing but clementine oranges. This rash lasted more than a month! But time was of the essence for me, so I had to detox fast. I am not suggesting this for anyone. Please be careful when changing your diet or coming off any medicine. It can be scary at times. I just went with it. I just wanted to live.

Becoming a Living Being

In his videos, Dr. Morse talked about a lot of other things besides health. In one video, he said that once you start eating raw, live food all the time you will start to "come alive." I really did not understand what he meant by that. I was already alive; well barely, but I was alive. What was he talking about? I was going to find out what he meant. Time marched on; it was the end of August or beginning of September, 2012. I started to be able to eat a bit more and I started eating salads at dinner time. I was talking to my dad one day about how I was eating raw, live, organic foods and I told him that a funny thing started happening to me: I had started to become so aware of everything. I started to feel like I was one with the plant that I was eating. I started to become aware of the birds in the backyard and the trees and all of nature around me. I was becoming "alive." It was as though these things started to "talk" to me in their own way. When you eat processed foods and cooked foods, it covers up the "junk" that we feel inside. This is why when you are sad or mad you reach for such types of food, or for drugs, or alcohol. It is all to cover up what you are really feeling inside. When you detox, you feel everything. It is physical as well as emotional. There is nothing to cover these things up. "We are just a bunch of cells and two fluids," Dr. Morse would say. "We need to feed ourselves live food in order for our cells to be alive." This was another aspect of waking up.

Hippocrates Was Right

Food is Medicine

HIPPOCRATES SAID, "Let food be thy medicine and medicine be thy food." I have learned that fruits are the healers within the food groups. Fruits have the highest magnetic energy and life force on this precious Planet, especially grapes and lemons. I know of someone who healed her chronic pain of seven years, with six months of eating and juicing just melons and she is thriving today and helping others, teaching them to help themselves how to heal. I have also heard that someone healed themselves from cancer on just grapes alone. Fruits are powerful in their energy. Vegetables are neutral in detoxing. Vegetables help you to even out a bit when detoxing gets too intense.

I have learned so much about so much since I started this sickness. I tell my friends that I feel like a walking book. These are just my opinions from the research that I have done. I would say that I spent at least 4 to 6 hours a day for over a year on research. I will just go over some of the things that I have learned. Some you may know and some you may not know, but I am finding out that there is so much more to this life than what we physically see or are taught to believe. Also, the industries that are out to make money are savvy at marketing and they play on our senses and emotions. We were brought up with them and we are emotionally attached to them, so it is hard to detach from them. This is part of the "programming" that has been instilled into us.

This is one of the first things I learned. Cow's milk is for baby cows, not humans. The way I understand this is that dairy products cause inflammation and most people do not have the enzyme in their bodies to digest it. It is filled with fat and everything a baby cow needs to grow. It does not do a body good. It actually depletes calcium from your bones. Your body needs to build up protection from the inflammation that cow's milk causes so once you eat or drink dairy, your body needs something to buffer the acids that it makes; one of the ways that it does this is that it sucks the calcium out of your bones. We do need calcium. You can get calcium from vegetable sources. I did not know this. There are many studies and articles on this. I know that dark leafy greens give you calcium, but we were brought up to believe that cow's milk is the best source for calcium. When given milk as a child, you didn't question it, you just drank it. Again, believing that dairy products during detoxing, or any other time, is not good for you is only my understanding from my research. Our bodies try to respond to eating dairy the best it can, but the less dairy you eat the better off you are. The industries want you to believe otherwise. The World lives on milk and cheese. My kids and husband drink almond milk now, but still eat pizza. We all need to learn on our own and in our own way. We all have our own journey to walk.

After my month of eating only watermelon, I then started my day with strawberries, blueberries, oranges, or grapes. Grapes and oranges actually got to be too much for me to handle. They would cause me to detox too fast. I was in enough agony as it was; I didn't need to feel worse. Strawberries and blueberries are what resonated with me so this is what I continued to eat. I also tried to eat the food that was in season. I have learned that we live in a blessed Universe. God put them here at the right time for the right reason. For example, berries are to be eaten in the summer. Berries taken internally are natural protection for your skin from too much sun. The sun is our friend and is essential for life. Some people actually sun gaze. I tried this for a little while, also. I was told, by the people on Dr. Morse's Facebook page, that it could regulate my sleep and that it harnesses a wealth of energy and power for me. As I was trying everything else that people were suggesting, I tried this as well. I was amazed that I could actually look at the Sun! If you are too acidic, you probably won't be able to. Once I was less acidic I was able to do this. Sun gazing has been around for a long time. If you are interested in this, just like anything else, please do your research first before you start. You could possibly damage your eyes if you don't do this correctly. When I started getting sick, I couldn't be in the sun for more than three minutes, or my skin would get extremely red and itchy. This was due to my acidic body reacting to the sun's rays that were attempting to love, detox and heal me. I didn't understand that at the time. We need the sunlight; it is a gift of the Universe and it is essential. I have heard that raspberry oil applied topically will protect you somewhat so that you won't burn; but the best way to protect yourself against too much sun is the shade.

After my month of watermelon, I started juicing apples and ginger every day. Raw apples are loaded with enzymes that help your stomach. Ginger helps the stomach as well. Then I started juicing apples, carrots, celery, and ginger every day. This is what I lived on. I would try to get my kids and husband to drink this as I knew it was the best thing for them, also. But at the time they were coming from a worse diet than mine had been. They would just say, "No thanks, we will leave it for you." They were kind of afraid of the new lifestyle that I had to adopt. I tried so hard to get them to listen to what I was saying about everything I was learning, but they weren't sick like me. I think they looked at it as if it was "sick food and drinks." I felt bad about how I let them just eat whatever they wanted; I really didn't understand how much it mattered what we ate. I was asleep at the wheel, so to speak.

Eating Raw, Organic, Fruits and Vegetables

As the months went on and I could finally stomach some different foods I tried some other raw foods such as dehydrated zucchini chips, and apple chips. I even made a raw apple pie and chocolate made with coconut oil, cacao powder, and maple syrup. I felt as though by adding a few more foods, I would fit into society a little better. Let's face it, not many people just eat raw organic fruits and vegetables and nothing else. My kids and husband also started to change the things they were eating and drinking somewhat. They even started drinking some of the juice!

When I told my mom what I was eating, I could just feel the sadness she felt in thinking that I couldn't eat anything else. But I needed to listen to my body and I did the best I could with it. At the time when I was just juicing, whenever I ate something instead of the juice, I would be completely exhausted. It was taking so much energy to digest my food that my body did not have energy to do any healing; I needed to avoid using energy for anything else but healing. As I look back, I think to myself that it took a lot of courage to trust a Doctor that I met on YouTube, but this is how powerful this man's energy and love for people was. He was truthful and you could sense it. He spoke about healing and peace. This was the beginning of the spiritual aspect of this whole experience.

Learning More

BPA

As I was continuing the process of eating, drinking and healing this way, I started to learn more about different aspects of health and what is unhealthy. One negative thing I learned was that there is a substance called bisphenol A (BPA) that we probably come into contact with every day. This chemical is in most plastic products and leaks into your food and drinks from bottles and cans. This chemical can behave in a similar way to estrogen and other hormones in the body. When your hormones are screwed up, your body is screwed up. BPA is in pretty much everything we use every day: water bottles, baby bottles, dental fillings, and sealants, dental devices, medical devices, DVDs, inside of food cans, etc. I went through my whole house and threw out anything that I found that contained BPA that we would put into our mouths. It just made me aware of what is right under our nose that is not good for us. Why would you put BPA in babies' bottles? BPA leaches more when plastic is heated in the microwave. I think we have all used microwaves once or twice. It is not good for you, but it is convenient. Everything today is about convenience. The lifestyle I was living was a huge change from convenience. The process that we had to go through each day and week was endless, but it was needed in order for me to have another day here. So this is what we did.

Our grocery process was an all-day affair. Once a week, my husband would go to the grocery store and buy all organic food. He would bring it home put it all away, then take the fruits and vegetables out again wash to it all, cut it up, and juice it. This "grocery process" from start to finish was about five to six hours. We filled both of our refrigerators up with fruits and vegetables so that we could have juice each day of the week. He or my children juiced for me every day. Juicing was a process that took at least over an hour every day. There was no skipping any days. It had to be done every day. There were no other options. This was my lifeline. It was my survival and they knew it and I knew it. It wasn't an easy road, for me or for them, but it was the road that showed up when nothing else did and I am so glad that nothing else did.

Body Just Wouldn't Work

I was in pretty bad shape and still wasn't working at our office. By this time I had asked my son Zachary not to go to college. I didn't want to do this, but I knew our business would be in rough shape if he didn't help. So I took on more guilt. I thought, "If I didn't get sick, then I wouldn't have to ask him to change his plans for the future." I felt awful asking this, but he didn't give it two thoughts. He said, "Of course I will stay home." Guilt is stifling. It is dead energy and will kill your body and your mind. Let go.

Gary and Zachary would help me in the mornings by juicing, and making sure I was warm enough before they left for work because I could not control my body temperature; I was freezing most days. I would have to take a couple baths a day to try to keep my body temperature at a level I could deal with. My body would only stay warm for a few hours at a time. It was maddening at times. I just wanted my body to work and it just wasn't.

I remember that a couple of times before Gary and Zachary left to go to work, Gary had to tie my arm to my body, then tie me to the chair at the kitchen table because my arms would just not work. They would hang there with no feeling; they were just dead weight. Since they didn't work, it was hard to hold myself up on the chair. It was the oddest feeling to have arms but be unable to use them because they didn't work. At this point, I felt as though I was never going to get better. It was just one thing after another.

During the fall and winter of 2012, I was at my worst point and my blood pressure dropped very low. When this sickness started my blood pressure was at 120/80. In my declining progression it dropped to around 80/50. I had very little energy, couldn't walk, could hardly talk; had no appetite, was very dizzy, had nausea, rashes, shortness of breath; my hair continued to fall out so much that I had to wear it short; I couldn't keep my body warm; I had lost 20 pounds, so I weighed about 100 pounds; I was extremely pale and looked like death. I also had breast lumps show up that I tried to shrink by placing castor oil packs on them. It was a tough time. I remember lying on the couch watching time go by. I would say to myself "I can live another five minutes"; the five minutes would go by and I would say it again, then again, until the hour went by. I did this a few times during the day when things were extremely bleak. I then started to be able to stretch it out to 10 minutes at a time. Things were not good at this time; but I did have some hope from listening to Dr. Morse say that eating fruit, taking herbs, and juicing would help me to get better. Even with that encouragement, it was difficult to keep up the hope.

I continued to eat the same way, continued taking herbs and continued juicing. I was starting to heal a bit more day after day. As I learned things, I started learning more about me. I had a lot of time on my hands, so I started researching things that people on Dr. Morse's Facebook page would mention. They would say things such as, "We are not just our bodies or our minds; we are much more." I did not understand this at all. These people talked about soul retrieval, twin flames, reiki, energy healing, etc. I started looking into these things on my own. I ended up doing my own soul retrieval. This is when part of your soul is left behind due to trauma in the past, most often when you were a young person. You need to go back to this time to reclaim the lost part of your soul, so that you can be whole again. I did this a few times. It did help, but I knew that I needed more healing.

Learning There Was Hope

Dr. Morse's Facebook page is always full of lovely souls and they are wealth of information. We discussed everything. At this time, because I was having trouble sleeping, I was learning about methods to help me sleep better, like EFT, NLP, Rick Simpson Oil, grounding, meditation, hypnosis, and more. I really didn't know what these things were, so I did more research.

I looked up EFT. EFT stands for "Emotional Freedom Technique." Many people call this "tapping." My definition of what this process does is that it brings body, mind, and spirit together. You physically tap on meridian points on the body. Meridian points are some of the same points on the body that are used for acupuncture. In tapping you are not using a needle; rather, you are physically tapping on these points to release emotion and get the Qi (Chi) moving. As you are physically tapping on these points, you say out loud what the problem is. You then continue to tap other meridian points on your body and you slowly switch from talking about the problem to talking about what you want to happen. There are many people who use this technique and there are many people who teach it. I have used this technique with Brad Yates. He has been on Oprah and Dr. Oz. I have tapped many times for different things: fear, negative thinking, my feelings about money, and especially sleeping. It has helped most times. I will continue to be grateful for the times when it has worked and also when it doesn't work; when unsuccessful, I know the cause has a lot to do with what I am not letting go of. There is much more to it, but this is basically how using this technique can help you to let go of things.

NLP is a process called Neural Linguistic Programming. What I learned from this was to actually tell myself that it is "safe for me to sleep." Truck drivers use this process because their sleep pattern is off so much. I have also used this process in addition to EFT for sleep. I learned that there was scientific evidence that says that NLP is a discredited pseudoscience. I didn't care about the science behind it. I just wanted to sleep.

The more EFT and NLP that I did, the more I felt that emotions were surfacing and I was letting go of things. For example, when you start to tap you say "Even though ____ (and then you state the problem)." In this case I sometimes said it was "hard to sleep and stay asleep; I love honor and accept myself." As you start the process, you say this three times as you tap with the "karate chop" part of your hand. As soon as I said this I started to cry. I had no idea why, though. Since I know that crying is cleansing to the body, mind, and soul, I knew it was a good thing to do so I continued with it. This was bringing all of me, together. It was a beautiful process to go through.

Herbs and All Plants Are Sacred

Rick Simpson Oil is Cannabis Oil. This is one of the most highly effective plants on the Planet. Have you ever wondered why there is so much controversy over it? Ask the government. I haven't gotten to the point yet in the story when I will tell you about Mother Mary coming to me, but I want to tell you what she said the other day. She is very wise. I am not. This message is not from me: I am not this clever. Also, if you quote anything from this book, I don't mind if you give me the credit for it; but if it is what Mother Mary, the Angels, or God has said, please give them the credit. They don't need it, but they deserve it and I am very protective of them. Mother Mary told me the other day, "God gives us tools on this Planet to use for healing. The plants, the trees, the leaves, the flowers, the herbs, the oils, the water, the rocks, the ground, and everything on this Planet is holy. Wherever you are, you should be taking off your shoes, because it is all holy ground."

This whole Planet, wherever you go, is holy ground! How cool is that???

We are too busy to see or understand this ... yet Facebook continues. Facebook does have its place in life. It is not good or bad, it's just what is.

Grounding

Something else I have learned that helps with sleeping is walking on the Earth barefoot. This is called grounding. This is a process of connecting your body to Mother Earth and her healing energy. This reduces inflammation and improves your health by the balancing of the electrons in your body. It is hard to do this in the winter, so Gary made me a grounding board for inside the house. There are many videos out there to show how to do this. He has an electrical background also, so it was easy for him. They having grounding mats and grounding sheets that you can buy to help you sleep. I am not sure if it will help you, but it has helped me.

I have also learned that you can visualize yourself dropping an anchor from your body deep into Mother Earth. You can tell yourself that it weighs a million pounds, because your brain doesn't know the difference between the thought of you having an anchor that weighs a million pounds or you holding a physical anchor that weighs a million pounds. This also helps tremendously to ground you.

Water is Alive

Researching things about health and herbs and what these natural substances could do for me, was my lifestyle now. I was trusting my God, who I have learned is also nature, to get me better. I have learned so much about herbs and natural remedies. This was the Universe telling me that I didn't need chemical substances to heal. The Earth has been equipped with everything I needed. So I stayed the course.

Throughout my researching, one thing always led to another. I was learning a lot about spiritual things. These spiritual things would meld into physical things to show me just how everything is connected. For example, I read about a person named Dr. Emoto. Dr. Emoto was interested in the molecular structure of water and what affects it. Water is the most receptive of the four elements of Earth, Air, Fire and Water. He did experiments that took water from the Fujiwara Dam and showed what the water looked like. Then he took that same water and had a Buddhist Monk bless it and it completely changed the molecular structure of it! It was as though it organized itself in love. He then took bottled water and taped words onto the bottles, and left them out overnight. He taped words like "Chi of Love," and "Thank You," and he also taped negative words on some of the bottles instead. It was as though the water molecules were accepting the love and in the same token would feel the negative words, also. The pictures from the bottle with the negative words on it showed the molecules looking physically sad. Please check out these pictures, they are amazing!! It is just another validation of how alive everything is and how everything needs love.

Dr. Emoto did another experiment with rice and water in Mason jars. He filled three Mason jars full of rice and water. He would say "I love you" to the first jar. To the second jar he would say "I hate you" and the third jar he would completely ignore. After a month, the first jar was looking fine and the rice was fermenting and smelling sweet. The second jar that he had said "I hate you" to was putrid and moldy, and the third jar was worse than the second jar. It was rotting away. The moral of all of this is that we need love and attention to not only survive, but to thrive.

Our bodies are made up of mostly water. Water is sacred, as are you. I bless my water before I drink it or use it, I say "I love you" to it and I say "thank you" to it. Water is a blessing.

Everyone Needs to Heal

Ho'oponopono Mantra and Music

MANTRAS ARE STATEMENTS that you continually repeat. By doing so, emotions are brought to the surface so that you can deal with them. I often listened to a Chi CD that my husband bought for me. It was a tranquil sound and as I sipped my Heal All Tea (this tea can be used for many ailments, from a toothache to a backache to a soother for a rash), I listened to this CD and start to draw. I didn't draw anything specific, but I felt the need to do something creative; I couldn't do much of anything else so I picked up a pen and started. It started with doodles and then became flowers. It was a creative outlet for me. As I drew, I cried. I did not understand this. So again, I went to the Internet to look up why I cried when I drew, and I was led to the Facebook page of Dr. M. I hope you understood that last part. Translation: we are led to things. We just need to be, and then follow what is brought forth. I was led to this mantra called Ho'oponopono meditation. This meditation is very simple. You simply continue to say I Love you, I am sorry, please forgive me, thank you I learned to say it the following way: I'm sorry, please forgive me, I love you, thank you; I am not sure why my guides wanted me to learn it this way, but this is what helped me to release things (at this time, I didn't know I had guides). For this mantra, you say these words to yourself over and over again. Let me just tell you, if you suspect you have past trauma inside of you that needs to come out, practicing this mantra will help it come to the surface. I did this several times, and yes, I cried a lot. I had no idea what I had inside. One thing we never run out of in my house is tissues! I cried all the time. I still do; it is very healing, so man or woman—cry—it is good for you! It means there is something inside that you need to deal with. Be grateful for whatever it was that brought the issues out and then let them go.

I then discovered that I also cried while listening to certain music. I couldn't understand this, either. My youngest son is a pretty good singer and he started to take singing lessons; and every time I heard certain tones come out of him, I cried. I couldn't help it. I think that he thought I was sad when he sang, so he stopped going to lessons. Again I started researching to find out why music made me cry. Music is very healing. Music is energy just like us. I found out that there is a 528 Hz tone. This is actually a tone of love. This tone miraculously cleaned oil-polluted water!! There is a lot of information available regarding this. These tones have been hidden from us for a long time. They are on the solfeggio scale.

There is also a 741 Hz tone on an A440 standard tuning scale that I have read about. I have learned that this is what most people listen to and it shuts down our chakras. We have seven major chakras. These seven major chakras make up our energy system. Each chakra has its own frequency and color and is located in certain spots on the body. It's hard to explain without showing you. Please do some research about chakras and what they do for us, as they are of major importance to our bodies. If these chakras are shut down, there is no energy flowing through them. This can lead to disease in the body. Again, there is a lot of information available if you want to learn more about this; I encourage you to do so, because it can help to heal us and heal our Planet. As you heal, the Planet heals, as we are one with it.

I Didn't Realize What Was Inside

In January, 2013, I started to do some small meditations, but something was telling me that I needed to do more meditating. It was a kind of knowing that kept telling me to "do more meditations." I ignored the instruction for a while as my conscious mind didn't think I needed to do more of this activity and my subconscious mind was programmed not to listen.

As I started to understand more of the aspects of my sickness, I gradually understood that this sickness was not just from me eating potato chips once in a while. It was becoming more obvious to me that there was some far greater purpose for all that had happened. I was learning so much already from the Internet and this kept me quite busy; not to mention, there wasn't much else that I was able to do. I was happy learning about all of these new topics, but then I started getting mad. As I learned more, I realized how many lies we are told constantly; and we are so asleep that we don't even see it. I was mad at GMO foods, I was mad that the bees were dying, I was mad that doctors are not taught much about nutrition and they are taught to just prescribe medication, that the government that governs our lands doesn't really care about us; and the list went on and on and on. I was starting to see just how mad I was. I was not only mad at things that were far separated from me, but also things that were close, such as our friends who didn't pay us our much-needed rent, people who took advantage of me in life, people who have lied to me, etc.; and that list, too, went on and on. I finally just started experiencing huge bouts of anger; so much so that I would need to go punch and scream into a pillow, day after day. I am a grown woman and looked very silly throwing tantrums, but I knew I needed to do this to get the anger out of me. I have now learned a much more sacred way to deal with my anger, but tantrums were the only way I knew how to do this at the time. I remember one day when I was so angry that I took my _iPad that I loved, as it connected me to the World that I was no longer a part of, and threw it across the room; it hit my bedroom wall next to where my husband was standing. I am so grateful that it didn't hit him. I screamed, "I can't do this anymore!" Gary came across the room to me, as I couldn't walk, and hugged me. He told me that things were going to get better. We still have the hole in the wall. Emotions get stuck in us, they get stuck in our cells, we hang on to them and they are stuck until we remove them somehow, someway. Be true to yourself. Say no, when you need to say no. You do not want to continue in life with anger inside of you. You will hurt yourself and possibly someone else. Been there, done that, cried and felt awful. (I am forever sorry, Valeria and Samuel, for the pain that I caused to both of you when we fought. I thank you for loving me through all of it. I didn't know how to love myself. I was dealing with me, and took it out on you. I know how to love myself now and I am here to invite others to learn to do the same. You have both allowed and assisted in this happening and are a big part of this book being written and going out to the World. Without your love and forgiveness it couldn't have happened this way. I am forever grateful to you.) Through this process I have learned that everything is sacred: the good, the bad and the ugly. Love yourself.

Dr. Sarika Arora

It was February of 2013, and after eight months of detoxing I was still on my diet of eating fruits and vegetables, as well as some other things every once in a while, but not much. I still had more healing to do, and I was thinking of getting my amalgam fillings out. These are mercury fillings in your mouth that constantly give out radiation which can also give you major problems. In researching who could do this for me in my area, I found Groton Wellness. This was about 30 minutes from me, and they also had a Farm to Table Café. I wanted to go there. Something drew me to it. They were having a special dinner there for Valentine's Day. Since I hadn't been out to eat in quite a while, I thought this would be a nice place for Gary and me to go to get local fresh food and have a date night. The food was unbelievably delicious. Paul was one of the chefs who came over to our table. He was so nice to us and I told him a little about my sickness and he told me that they had Naturopathic doctors there. I was thrilled to know that someone in my area was helping to heal people the way that I learned to heal myself. The following week I made an appointment with Dr. Arora. She is a functional medical doctor. Her philosophy was that she believed in the body healing itself. This is what I believed in also, as I had lived it, thus far. I made an appointment with her for March, 2013. During my appointment she wrote down everything as I spoke. She was interested in everything that I had gone through and was going through. She cared. She did an examination, but more importantly, she listened to me. She wanted me to get my emotions out and she let me cry as she wrote down all my symptoms. I had some blood tests done and I found out at this time that I was not producing any pregnenolone , which is a hormone that is responsible for making a lot of other hormones. Remember when I said that when your hormones are messed up, you are messed up? Well I wasn't kidding. Dr. Arora told me that I had detoxed enough and started me on supplements and wanted me to start incorporating other foods. So, long story short, she also has been a big part of me getting better. The lack of pregnenolone was a part of the physical or scientific reason that I was sick, but there was something beyond science causing me to be sick. I would later find out more about this.

I had a couple of appointments with Dr. Arora during

March and April of 2013. At one of these appointments, I was telling her that I was having a lot of panic attacks. She encouraged me to do some breath work. This sounded strange to me. I didn't realize that the way you breathe is important. She told me that this would help me and told me how to practice a specific breathing exercise: she wanted me to breathe in for four seconds, hold my breath for seven seconds, and let it out for eight seconds. She wanted me to do this ten times, twice a day, once in the morning and once in the afternoon. I started to do this. It really helped with my anxiety. I hadn't realized that at times I just wasn't breathing very much. This type of breathing helps your nervous system calm down, without the use of drugs. How about that? This type of breathing also helps you to detox and also helps with many other things. Breathing patterns are important, especially in meditation. God gives us breath. When you breathe you are actually breathing in and out your life force energy. In essence, you breathe in and out God. Please look into this also, as it can only help you, and in turn, help Mother Earth.

Qi Gong

Dr. Arora wanted me to also start exercising once I felt up to it. This took a couple months more, but once I felt that I could do something more than just sitting there and doing nothing, I started to do Qi Gong exercises. This is a series of stretching movements that also help detox the body. It also helps to detox the mind and soul (I didn't know this at the time). These are subtle movements that flow. I still didn't have much energy, so I started to do this while sitting on a chair. Once I could do these movements effectively sitting down, I tried to do them while standing up. I couldn't stand for long, but I did what I could. When I moved my arms together and apart I started to notice something. I could actually feel the energy between my hands when I did some of these movements. I researched this, and found that we indeed have our own "Chi" energy. I found a video on YouTube that showed someone taking a small piece of square-shaped paper, folding it corner to corner so that it made four even triangles and put the center of the square paper on the head of a pin. The pin was stabilized by placing it through a book of matches. The person conducting this experiment would then take his hands and show that the Chi energy that we have will move the paper in a circle without touching it!! You just place your hands around it, but don't touch it and it moves!! I had to try this, so I did and it moved with my energy! I started to learn more and more about how our bodies have this energy, and it finally led me to understand that this is what we are all made of, energy.

In doing Qi Gong, I learned more about the spiritual side of life.

While doing research, I saw words like chi energy, energy healing such as reiki, soul retrieval, past lives, lightworkers, indigo and crystal children and more. These were definitely calling to me. I needed to find out more about all of these things. Therefore, more research was in order.

Then, I Heard From Heaven

Hearing from Heaven

THINGS WERE PROGRESSING slowly but steadily for the next few months. Then I started to have a lot more trouble sleeping. This also lasted for a few months. This is now slowly getting better as I learn more about what I am here to do. I had so much difficulty sleeping, that I hated for the night to come. I lay awake and listened to everyone sleeping around me. This was also maddening. This was actually a key turning point in my story. One morning, in August of 2013, I had just gotten out of bed after not sleeping the night before. It was about 5 a.m. I was enraged. I hated not sleeping. I told Gary I needed to leave the house. He asked me where I was going at 5 a.m. I said, "I don't know. I just need to leave." I limped to my car and got in. My plan was to slam into a telephone pole. I just wanted it over. I didn't want to go through this anymore. As I pulled out of my driveway, I could feel the rage surfacing. I stepped on the gas harder and harder. The telephone pole was coming closer and closer. I was screaming to God, "Okay, is this it? Am I going to die today?" I was screaming and crying and just didn't want to live anymore. And then all of a sudden a calmness overtook me. I don't know if it was the Angels, my spirit guides, God, Jesus, Mother Mary, or my higher self, and at this time, I was not communicating with any of them yet—but something told me, "No, this wasn't it. You have a life to live. You have importance here with Gary and your boys. They all need you. Go home." So that is what I did. I came into the house sobbing, telling Gary what had happened. He just hugged me and told me that things were going to get better. Did I mention that he is a saint?

You Matter

Loving Yourself Is Where the Answers Are

I T WAS THE END of August, 2013, and I was still having insomnia troubles. I saw that someone had posted something on Facebook about Louise L. Hay and her book, *You Can Heal Your Life*. The funny thing is that I had bought this book several years earlier but had never read it. A month or so before seeing the Facebook post, I saw a video with her in it and she was talking about the "law of attraction"; I loved learning about this topic, so again I was drawn to the book. It also taught me about how important positive affirmations are. I started to repeat the positive affirmations suggested in this book. I started to tell myself that I loved myself. And yes, I cried and cried. I just couldn't look in the mirror and say this. It was like my soul and my body and mind were all different things. I couldn't accept myself. When you are like this, you have a lot of work to do.

So I would continue each day with the positive affirmations and it started to change the old programming that I had in my brain. When a bad thought about me came into my head, I would just say that's a lie and I would back it up with a positive affirmation. And this continued for weeks. As soon as it started to set in, that I was a beautiful human being and that I deserve things just like everyone else, my life just started changing very rapidly. I wrote a list of what I deserved; the list was not written in an egotistical way or in a way that I was harboring anger, such as, "I think I am better than everyone else and I'm gonna get mine." Rather, it was from my soul; it was a gentle, "I am a human being, I am loved and I deserve" ... and the list kept going and going. I realized that I had been feeling that I didn't deserve friends, a husband like Gary, love, health, forgiveness, etc. I certainly didn't feel like I was worthy enough for God to love me or worthy enough to be communicating with His Angels. I felt as though I wasn't worth the cost of getting better. This is what the World is suffering from right now: we just don't feel worthy. The feelings of worthlessness went pretty deep. It went as far as not wanting to take up space on the Planet. I am not sure where this feeling originated, but my brain programming believed that I didn't deserve anything in this World, so I did not want to take up someone else's space on the Planet. This thinking can make you very sick. You can carry prior hurts with you for a very long time. Go inside, find it, and let it go. You deserve to allow yourself to live life to the fullest. This is why life was given to us, to live it to the fullest.

I wasn't resonating with any of these things at the time, so instead I started to repeat many positive affirmations such as, "I am beautiful, I am a wonderful friend, I have lots of money, I sleep soundly every night," as these were what I chose to affirm. I repeated these things over and over again. You can choose whatever you want in life. The Law of Attraction was working. I started to see that I did deserve whatever I wanted in life and I didn't even need to know how it was going to happen. I only needed to know that I *deserved* to know and it made all the difference. You are a deserving human being.

I was seeing firsthand what my life had brought me to. All of my experiences and challenges in life brought me to this point and I am very grateful for them all, because without them I would not be where I am today. It was not easy. Rites of passage never are. Our biggest challenges are our greatest teachers.

Using Your Intuition

Thomas Edison often sat in a chair and held ball bearings until his muscles got tired; this is the point at which he asked questions about his inventions, and answers came to him. Albert Einstein stared at the clouds and he asked questions, and answers would come. Nikola Tesla had blueprints in his mind so clear that he didn't usually have to write them down. All knowledge already exists in the Universe. You just need to quiet your mind, ask questions, listen, and believe what you are hearing. These people all knew this. They knew themselves and believed in themselves. This is also essential.

This is what I now try to instill into my children: you do not need to plan your life and plan how you are going to make things happen. You just need to know that you deserve to have a wonderful life and you will, if this is what you have in your thoughts. You will attract this into your life. Once you realize that you have the map to you, and you are the driver and the Universe is the road, there is no stopping you from accomplishing whatever you are to do here on this Planet. I also tell them that they don't need to further their education in college if they do not feel led in that direction. I know this isn't for everyone. I don't want them to go, just to go. Right now it is not the time to acquire a bill that will be very hard to pay off, especially if you don't like what you are doing. I am trying to teach them to listen to their intuition, to understand that money is not the most important thing. It is a tool. If you feel called to go to a certain college or the Marines or sports camp, then by all means, go. Go for you. Learn for you. Live life for you. We are all on our own path in life. School is learning; being in the work force and learning on your own is a type of learning, also. You should never stop learning about whatever interests you, as this is your soul speaking. Never stop learning. I think they get the message. This is loving yourself.

The Universe and the
Angels Answered

These People Just Showed Up

AT THE END OF August or beginning of September 2013, I was able to walk a little more easily without limping so much; it was intermittent but at least I was standing and walking a little more on my own. It felt amazing to stand on both legs at the same time and not fall over! It felt miraculous to feel that I had strength in both legs at the same time. After you haven't walked for a while as soon as you get back to it, you feel like a new person. I continued with my Qi Gong and I started to practice Yoga as well. I was looking up videos on Yoga and was led to see a video that told me about Hay House Radio. I couldn't get on my phone fast enough to download this. I started to listen to it. I was drawn to this. As I started listening to everyone on Hay House radio I couldn't get enough of all these people, every day. Wayne Dyer, Louise L. Hay, Denise Linn, Dr. Mona Lisa Schultz,

Darren Weissmann, Dr. Christine Northrup, Cheryl Richardson, Michael Bernard Beckwith, Gerry Gavin, Doreen Virtue and the list went on and on. They were in my "frequency" so to speak. These people helped change my life, especially Wayne Dyer. I feel like we are the same level in our hearts. It is crazy how close I feel to all these people and I don't know any of them personally. It is what they give from their hearts and I feel it in mine. It is an awakening! I was being awakened and they were all on this journey with me (in my opinion, Hayhouse and all those involved with them are the cornerstone of this awakening movement.)

I believe that this was what my sickness was all about. At the time that I started getting sick, the Planet started to really shift into this time of change. There is a spiritual shift going on and I have been chosen to be a part of this, by writing about what it is really all about.

There was a rapid progression in my sickness and equally there has been a rapid progression in my awakening. I continued to listen to Hay House Radio. They talked about things like: God, past lives, spirit guides, Angels, people who have crossed over, and basically how to live here on this Earth plane being a spiritual being in a human body. My belief system was not equipped to handle all this information at once. I had to take one thing at a time, but the more I listened, the more I understood, and the more information I wanted. It was a thirst from my soul.

Asking for Proof

I heard from Doreen Virtue and others that we had guardian Angels. I knew that the Bible talked about Angels, but I wasn't quite sure that we all actually had them. Were we that special that we each had guardian Angels? Doreen discussed the Angels in detail. I decided to look into this further. I researched the topic and found that other people on YouTube had asked their Angels for proof that they were there. They advised others to ask for something from the Angels that is not of the ordinary; in this way, there would be no doubt that the Angels were showing you proof that they are with you. I thought, "This can't be true, can it?" I thought to myself, "What could I ask for?" I said, "Okay, Angels, could you please show me that you are here by showing me a green cat." Yes, a green cat. I was looking all over my house for any signs of a green cat. I didn't see any. I was thinking that maybe it was too strange a request. I was also thinking, "Where is a green cat going to come from?" I gave up looking around my house for one. It was a nice day so I thought I would go for a drive. As I drove my car, I still watched for any sign of a green cat and nothing turned up. No sooner had I said, "Okay, forget it," when I looked over on the left hand side of the road and in the driveway of one of my neighbor's house was a huge stuffed green cat in the trash pile! Yes, that was my green cat. I flipped out a little bit and turned around to look again. I took a picture and went home and thanked the Angels and lit a candle. This wasn't the end of my Angels. This was just the beginning. That day I sat on the driveway with our puppy, Bella. It is not my habit to just sit in the driveway, but this day I did and I was sitting right in front of a 10-foot–long, wide crack and right in front of me where I was sitting was a feather. It could have been anywhere in that crack, but it was right in front of me!

Angels Try to Get Your Attention

I have been told that the Angels will try to get your attention by showing you other things that have to do with them, be it names or numbers. This is exactly what was happening. I walked into my garage and on a box on the floor it said in big letters "Angels." My full name is Angela Mia which means "my angel" in Italian. I collected Angels over the years and that was one of the boxes that contained Angels. I walked by the box every day for years and I never noticed this.

My son Cody has a friend named Angel who he had just started to hang around with, and his school teacher's first name is Angel. They were trying to get my attention.

The next day I needed to pick up Cody at school for an appointment. I was on cloud nine as I went to the school, because all this had happened with the Angels the day before. I went into the office and there was a notice about a benefit for the 26 Angels who left us on December 14, 2012, in Newtown, Connecticut. Then something else was happening to me. I kept hearing these voices in my heart; each time someone new came into the office, I heard different names come to me. I brushed this off, as I was so happy to know that my Angels were talking to me. I realized that there was more that they were trying to get me to see. We went home and I was talking to Cody about the feathers and everything else that had happened with the Angels; I got out of the car and started to walk up my driveway and right in front of me another feather fell. It didn't just fall, it actually swooped, and it wasn't big. It could have swooped anywhere, but it happened to swoop right in front of me so that I could catch it! There was nothing in the sky as far as we could tell. I was elated; I was so happy and crying all at the same time. I was seeing that they wanted my attention and they were getting it.

I even found a feather in my car. My car was locked and the windows were completely shut and on the floor in the back seat there was a feather! The night before this, four boisterous boys were in the back seat after a basketball game. It could have flown out of the car at any time that they got out, but it was there on the floor of the backseat when I got into the car the next morning! I just laughed! They were real and they were leaving me feathers everywhere, so that I would know they were there.

We Are All Capable of "Tuning In"

I continued to listen to people on Hay House Radio, such as John Edward and James Van Praagh; these two men are mediums. I listened to what they were saying and they always said that anyone can do this; we are all capable of being mediums. I did not believe in mediums, and also I interpreted the Bible as saying that this was wrong; therefore, I did not think that I myself could have this happen. How could I hear someone who has passed to the other side?

Of all the people I listened to on Hay House Radio, Wayne Dyer has been the most impactful for me. I had watched Wayne on the PBS channel every once in a while but only for a few minutes; then I would turn the channel. I was not ready yet for the impact that he would have on me. Wayne is one of those people who you can sense has something peaceful and different about him, but you just aren't sure what it is about him that draws you to him. For me, he was just like Dr. Morse. I began listening to this man; and it seemed that I hung onto everything he said with both hands. In one of his videos, he explained how he studied the Tao Te Ching. This is teaching from Lao Tzu. This is the most famous and translated work from the Taoists. It is pure consciousness. It consists of 81 short chapters among which 37 form the first part, the *Book of the Way* (tao) and the next 44 form the *Book of Te*. The way I remember he explained it was that he took a year to study the work and he did this by taking each verse for 4 days and applying it to his life. He wasn't doing this for profit or for his ego; he was doing this because he was hearing his own spirit call to him. This is what is going to change our World. When you improve yourself, you put that out to the Universe and it improves others, as we are all connected. That is what Wayne has been dedicated to doing. I was so impressed by this; but beyond being impressed, there was also something about his spirit that I just needed to know more about.

Hearing the Angels

The Angels were not just leaving me feathers all the time; they were also starting to talk to me. I know it sounds crazy, but they were. I was driving down the street one day and I kept hearing, "No Judgment, No Judgment, No Judgment." Anything that I would think about, as petty as it may have been, the voice said, "No Judgment." I started to listen. We all have lots of judgments about many aspects of life. When you judge others you are judging yourself, and that prevents healing. I started hearing many suggestions, so I wrote them down. This is a very small list of what the Angels told me:

Let it Be, Just Be, Just Love, Just Heal, Just Laugh, Just Smile, Just Live, Be Still and Hear God, We are Here, No Fear, We are One: phrases all very simple and sweet.

As time went on, I gained more and more understanding. I looked into the sky and Angels appeared in cloud-form in the sky. I have these pictures. One day I was lying on my couch and looked out the window into my backyard. I lay on this same couch day after day when I was sick and looked out the same window. This particular day,

I was looking at the trees and I actually saw physically that there were Angels in the trees, lifting their wings to the Heavens. They looked like they were praising God! My son Cody and I took pictures of this and we noticed that in the pictures what appeared to be a cross right above the head of one of these Angels. What I realized from this is that these Angels were watching over me the whole time while I was sick and I hadn't even known it. I am here to tell you that they are with you. All the time. They watch over us, all of us. I was starting to notice a lot more things now. My eyes were opened. I questioned why this was happening. Why me? I had many questions.

Everything Was Lining Up

At my next appointment with Dr. Arora., I explained to her about how I was doing. I tried to tell her about all of what was happening to me. She told me that she was seeing a Shaman in Boston named Kate and that she wanted me to speak with the Shaman. My doctor was talking to me about spiritual things! I was elated that she didn't want to put me in a straightjacket after hearing what I was telling her. She gave me Kate's number and email, so I called Kate the next day and left a message. After not hearing back by a few days later, I called her again. I waited a few more days and there was still no response. I emailed her and no response. Probably two weeks went by without hearing anything. I emailed Dr. Arora on November 14th and told her that I had not heard from Kate the Shaman. The following day November 15th, Kate sent me an email. I didn't see it until the next day, which was November 16th, which was the day of the Natural Living Expo in Marlboro. How blessed I was that this was in my own city. The night before the expo Gary had printed out a list of all the booths that were going to be there so that I could make sure we visited the ones most important to me of the 225 booths! I was looking at the packet of all the booths that would be at the show and making a checkmark next to the booths I wanted to visit. I finally read the email from Kate on the day of the expo. She told me that she was not accepting any clients, but asked me what my situation was. So I gave her the fast version: I got sick a year and a half ago, no one can tell me why, I am better, and now I am talking to Angels and getting feathers. She said that she highly recommended that I go to see Karen Paolino. Karen is an Angel reader and she has a place in Pembroke, Massachusetts, called Heaven on Earth. I was crying when I read this. Why, you ask? Because Karen was going to be at the show THAT DAY and it was one of the booths that I had checked off. I hadn't heard anything from this woman for weeks and the day she gets back to me was the same day that I was going to see the woman who she highly recommended that I see! I just wanted to find someone who could tell me why this was all happening. I went outside after reading that and I asked aloud, "Is this what I am supposed to do?" On the ground was a beautiful, fluffy gray feather. I hadn't been receiving feathers for a little while and this was on the ground right in front of me on top of the snow! I cried. This was my answer!

We went to the expo and had a wonderful time! And to think I wasn't going to go, until my wonderful husband suggested that we see it. When I was at the expo I felt like I was home. It was as though I had come home to the mother ship! It was amazing!! One thing I noticed was that a lot of it was about healing. I didn't understand this. It was as though they knew I was coming and they wanted to teach me how to heal myself on all levels. These people could look into my soul and they knew what I was going through. Love and unity knows love and unity, and that is what I was experiencing. There were psychics, reiki healers, angel readers, holistic healing, whole foods, crystal booths, singing bowls, mantras, and all kinds of metaphysical booths, and so much more. I was intrigued to say the least. While I was there, among other experiences, I had my Aura picture done and I saw the spirit guides there with me. I really didn't understand much of this, but I knew I was in the right place. I went to Karen's booth and she told me to go to her seminar. I did this. In her seminar, she explained that we should ask the Angels to know what our life purpose is, to have them show each of us and put the synchronicities into place. That day I began to notice the synchronicities in my life, and I have been aware of them since that day.

Angel Readers

I went to two other Angel readers at the expo and while listening to the first one, I cried so much that I couldn't even hear her or really pay attention to what she was saying. So, later in the day, I went to see another of the angel readers. Her name is Chris Alexandria. She was very practical as she read my Angel cards. She helped me so much that I brought my son Anthony to see her the next day. I also noticed that on her logo was the filigree design that I continued to draw each time I listened to Hay House Radio. More synchronicities.

The feathers continued; I remember that I asked for them and they just appeared on the ground in my path. Some days just one, some days eight! I was always brought to tears; I was elated that the Angels were there and were listening to me. The Angels are there for everyone and they talk all the time. Our lives are just way too busy to sit quietly and hear them. If you would like to hear them, start with meditation; even if it is for only a few minutes. Meditation can help you get to know the Angels, and they you, and it also helps you to know yourself. All knowledge is inside of you.

Starting to Experience My Awakening

Mom and Dad

MY MOM AND DAD always checked in on me to see how I was feeling. By this time they had noticed that I had made great progress. I decided to talk to my mom and dad about what was happening to me. So every once in a while I let them know how things were progressing. They both believe in Angels. My mom says she hears them in the morning when it is quiet. This was very comforting to me, as it meant I was in good company. She also believes that mediums are real and believes in other aspects of intuition. My dad told me that Bishop Sheen talked about Angels. He ordered for me the DVD and I watched it. Bishop Sheen was very popular back in that day. They believed in what I told them and that was such a blessing to me. I couldn't deny all that was happening in my life, and their belief in me meant that I didn't have to try to deny it.

One day Gary and I went to visit my dad and he gave me a book that he had gotten as a gift for his birthday a couple years previously. It was Doreen Virtue's book on Arch Angel Michael! I was astonished that he would know Doreen Virtue or Arch Angel Michael, as they were part of my new family on Hay House Radio. He told me that at his church they routinely ask Arch Angel Michael to protect them. He gave me the prayer that they say every service. We also started discussing other spiritual people who were familiar to us. He was talking about some saints who I had never heard of. I asked him who the nun was in the movie who was limping at the end of it. I remembered watching this several years ago with my stepdad and it was resonating with me for some reason. It was one of his favorite movies and he is a war movie kind of guy. I needed to know who that was. It was a thirst to know. I would eventually find out who it was and why I had felt such a thirst to know.

The next day, in searching for information on YouTube about Doreen Virtue, I learned that she went to Lourdes in France, where St. Bernadette saw the Immaculate Conception 18 times. I was reading about this and realized that *this* was who I had asked my dad about the day before! It was St. Bernadette! And Doreen Virtue wrote a book about the healings in Lourdes, France, via Mother Mary. I didn't understand at the time why I needed this information, but it turned out that it is very significant in my life. The synchronicities were accumulating at a rapid rate now. The words "Let It Be" often appeared to me out of nowhere. I heard it from the Angels, it was on a tea bag, or I heard the song, or it was on something that my kids showed me. It was getting comical. One day I was shopping in a store down the street from me. I walked through most of the aisles, except one that I had not planned to go down; but something brought me to it. I started looking at the items on the shelf and there I saw a letter-holder with the words "Let It Be" on it! Why on a letter holder? I have no

idea, but I knew it was for me to see. I have come to simply know things. My husband played the song one night for me in the car, as he had heard me singing it that day; I couldn't stop crying once it started to play. I would one day find out why this was so significant to me.

Meeting Monya, My Soul Sister

I still didn't have anyone in my life to explain all of this to me. I really thought I might be losing my mind. Then one day my son Anthony's best friend, Brett, was saying that his mom goes to a spiritual circle once a month and all she does is cry. Well, crying is right up my alley, so I said, "I have to know where she goes." I got in touch with Jen, who is Brett's mom, and she got in touch with the woman who holds these circles; the woman has studied under four Shamans. Her name is Monya. Monya agreed that I could get in touch with her. It was a Friday afternoon that I spoke to her and she said she could see me that evening! I asked Gary to join me, and he obliged. As soon as I walked down her stairs, I started crying. She had crystals and feathers and artifacts and a huge painting that she painted at the bottom of the stairs. I started crying just looking at it. She asked me what I felt or saw and I told her that I saw me. I had no idea what the source was, but I felt the energy or sadness of the painting. I walked into the sacred space and again, cried. We spoke for four hours. During our conversation she asked me what had happened to me when I was three. She was also a medium. I asked, "Holy-moly, how do you know that?" It kind of scared me. She just looked up and said, "I am just the channel." I proceeded to tell her that I had had my right kidney removed when I was about three. The kidney had a congenital defect, which means that it had been defective since birth. Monya told me that in communities that include a Shaman, the indication that someone is meant to be on the path of a Shaman is a congenital defect; hence, me.

As we continued to talk, I kept hearing the names Dan, Dan, Daniel, and John and John Son or Johnson. I had to ask her, "Who is Dan?" She said, "Dan is my father." We had just been talking about her father; then I asked, "And who is Johnson?" She just looked at me again and said, "John is the father of my son, Scotty." Scotty had passed away six years prior to this. I was picking up on Scotty's energy. And Gary picked up on me saying Johnson. He said "No, Ang, it's 'John's son.' Like son of John." Scotty was John's son. I was pretty scared again at that point. It brought me back to when I was at the school in the office and names kept coming to me. I was becoming a medium among all the other things. The painting at the bottom of the stairs was painted by Monya in Scotty's honor. I was picking up on Scotty's energy there. Monya explained to me that I have been experiencing my awakening. All of what I had been going through was all part of an awakening to the reality of what really is and what we really are. It was a powerful night. Gary got to see and experience me doing this. He said he would have had a hard time otherwise believing it if he hadn't been there to witness what had happened.

December 16, 2013 – First Angel Sighting

My friendship with Monya continued and she told me that she wanted to help me; she would take me under her wing, so to speak. I wrote down topics that I would like to discuss with her and then we talked about all of them. One thing I told Monya is that my house felt as though there were presences in it. I told her that while talking with the

Angels, I may have let some presence into my house without meaning to. This definitely can happen, so please be sure you ask for Arch Angel Michael's protection always! Monya suggested that she come to the house and clear it for me and my family. She taught me how to call in the directions and ask for protection, and she proceeded to clear the house. It felt so much better after she did this. I just love Monya!

Only a couple days went by before I had my first Angel sighting! Yes, I actually saw the Angel. I was sitting at the computer, like I am right now, and out of the top corner of my left eye was a beautiful brilliant gold light. It was small, bright, and fast. The Angels will only give me as much as I can handle. There was so much happening for me at this time, that I think they did not want me to "lose it." They will one day show themselves to me when I can take it all in.

Following the Spiritual Breadcrumbs

As I researched something, whatever it was, it drew me to the next subject I was to learn about. There were so many of these synchronicities happening that I just can't recall them all. I feel as though my life has been planned out already. I only need to follow the breadcrumbs or just remember. It is as though I was told what I was going to be learning for the day; it was almost like the Heavens were saying, "Welcome to class Angela. Sit here and we will be studying ____ subject today as it will come up in your life in the next 24 hours." It really makes me just laugh sometimes. Laughter is also healing. I read about a man who healed himself on laughter alone!!

In my researching that day, a man called "John of God" kept coming up. I also was hearing mention of John of God on websites and on YouTube. I had no idea who John of God was, but I knew that since he kept coming up I was soon to learn about him. John was a man in Brazil who has said that great doctors and even King Solomon would enter him, and through them, he performed healings and even live operations. As I understood it, all these procedures were without anesthesia or antibiotics. The incisions, to most people, feel like a paper cut: they don't bleed very much and there is rarely an infection. John of God has been studied by many people. There is no scientific explanation for what he is doing to help people. All day long I watched videos on this man. Something came to me that night and brought the knowledge that John of God can heal because he has the same Hz frequency as light. The next day as I was watching the YouTube video on this man again, a doctor was on the website and said pretty much the same thing as what had come to me in my sleep! I was amazed that I would just know such information. But I did. And it wasn't because I had heard it before on this Earth plane. It came to me in the middle of the night, woke me up until I wrote it down. Then I went back to sleep the best I could. I had a feeling it would have some significance. It certainly did!

Being Guided

Wayne Dyer and John of God

IN LISTENING TO Wayne Dyer on the day following this, I heard him say that he had been diagnosed with leukemia. On hearing this, I wanted to find out how he was doing because I love Wayne so much; so I searched for information about his leukemia. On one of his broadcasts, I heard him talk about a healing with John of God! Wait a minute, did he just say JOHN OF GOD? Yes, he did. Wayne explained that he had a friend who suggested that he see John of God. Wayne was told what he needed to do to prepare for this long distance surgery (yes, you read correctly, it was long distance surgery). He did as he was instructed: he was required to take herbs for a little while before the surgery and he needed to wear white. Wayne was in one part of the World and John was in another and John performed long distance surgery on Wayne. Wayne thought that after his "spiritual surgery" he would be able to go for a walk, as he is normally quite active. He was told that he would need to go back to bed for 24 hours. Wayne was taken aback by this. He said, "What do you mean, back to bed? I just got up and the surgery isn't even hands-on surgery—it's done from thousands of miles away!" John performed the surgery at 7 a.m. At 7:30 the surgery was over and Wayne tried to go for a walk shortly after this. He got about 100 feet and collapsed onto the ground. He needed to go back to bed for 24 hours. His son asked him what was wrong with his eye. It looked as though he had no pupil and it was extremely red like someone scratched his face. One of the things that John of God is told to do in his healings is scraping the eye. Wayne needed to go back to bed for that 24 hours. His kids were there to take care of him while he recovered. Now he believes his leukemia is gone, and he doesn't need tests to convince him; he believes we are what we think. I believe this, too.

Remember how I said that Wayne was such an influence on me? Well, I was telling my mom and dad that I was going to get them books from Wayne and give the books to them for Christmas. I did get my mom a book of his and got my dad the *Experiencing the Miraculous* DVD set. These were DVDs of Holy places that Wayne went. These were places my dad told me about years ago. These places are Lourdes, France where St. Bernadette saw Mother Mary; Medjugorje in Bosnia, where Mother Mary has been appearing for 28 years; and Assisi in Italy where St. Francis lived and where Wayne felt the presence of St. Francis while he was speaking about him. There is no separation.

We are one with the saints, also. When I was younger, I didn't know much about St. Francis except that he was Catholic; the way I was taught to believe while being in the nondenominational Protestant church was that Catholicism was wrong, and therefore, St. Francis was wrong as was Mother Theresa. This was my belief system at the time. No blame on anyone's part; it was just what I was taught, what I learned and believed for a time. I now know a lot more. To me it is about a person's heart. Both of these souls had incredible love in their hearts for people and animals. Anyway, I bought the DVDs for myself, also, and I started to watch them. In the video, Wayne explained who St. Francis was. He spoke very highly of him and described that St. Francis was full of love: he loved animals and people so much that he kissed lepers on the mouth, and he communicated with the birds and all of nature as this is where he saw that God was; and he was also devoted to the poor and the lame. I wept, because I felt very ashamed that I had shrugged off St. Francis without even knowing who he was and what he was about, simply because I associated him with the Catholic faith. Again, I am learning from my mistakes. What a blessing it is to know that making mistakes can be as powerful as not making them. It is all good. I am no longer a part of any "religion." I am for love. My mom told me that the new Pope took his name from St. Francis. I love this new Pope. He is a Pope of the people. He is a man full of love and grace and he shows it not just to Catholics, but to everyone. He has a wonderful heart just like St. Francis. I learned about St. Francis and who he really is from watching Wayne's DVD. Earlier in life, while growing up in the Catholic faith, I learned the prayer of St.

Francis from my mom and dad. When we were younger, my brother and sisters used to say this prayer before bed. I never really listened and understood this prayer. I do now.

It is as follows:

Lord make me an instrument of thy peace. Where there is hatred, let me sow love; where there is injury, pardon; where there is doubt, faith; where there is despair, hope; where there is darkness, light; where there is sadness, joy. Oh Divine Master, grant that I may not so much seek to be consoled, as to console; to be understood as to understand; to be loved as to love; for it is giving that we receive; it is in pardoning that we are pardoned; and it is in dying that we are born to eternal life.

I said this prayer as a young girl. I wasn't awake enough to understand this prayer. I now finally understand what St. Francis was talking about. He was enlightened and he was completely about love. This is what I feel that I am being led to. I have recently been told that my spirit guides are the Saints; I can definitely feel that one of these is St. Francis.

Healing Entities

Early the next morning after learning about St. Francis, my son Cody woke up feeling nauseous. I asked my husband to go into the bathroom with him, as I don't do well when the kids are nauseous. I had hurt my back a week before that and it was bothering me so much that had been sleeping on the floor. I went back to sleep on the floor and as I was lying there I felt this "presence" enter into my feet then settle into my body. It felt calm, subtle, and like a healing entity, so I wasn't frightened by this feeling. I have had other entities merge with me in the past and they weren't as friendly. This spirit didn't feel like that, so I was okay with it. It told me to go to Cody in the bathroom and it proceeded to tell me where to place my hands on him. It wasn't just on his stomach but on his back, too. I did this. I had him lie down on the floor and I proceeded with what I had been instructed to do; then the knowledge of where to put my hands on him in order to heal him just came to me. I proceeded to do this with a good amount of pressure. Cody is a sensitive kid and I would not normally use this much pressure, but this is what I had been told to do. It was as if I didn't have a choice, but not in a forceful way. This continued for about an hour until he fell into a deep sleep. He woke up a couple hours later, not feeling nauseous anymore. I texted Monya and asked her about entities with healing powers entering one's body. She called me and talked me through the whole experience. She told me that the body has meridian points and that I was probably told to go to these points on his body. At this time, I had no idea where the meridian points are. I was told to go to these points on his whole body, his arms, legs, hands, head, back, and stomach. She said that my gifts are occurring at a rapid rate. That afternoon I was extremely exhausted. I was hesitant to tell Gary about this, but I did tell him; I also told him that I had talked to Monya about all of this and she said that not a lot of people have the gift of laying on of hands but it sounded like an explanation of what had happened. Oh yeah, my back pain went away, also. When you heal others, you yourself are healed. Crazy stuff, huh? No, I need to change that word crazy to joyful. Joyful stuff, huh?

My Angel feathers were not coming anymore; my mindset was that I know they are here with me now, I don't continually need reminders. They are always awesome to get but by this time, there was a good amount of snow on the ground. I just tried to carry on and "do the dance" as Monya puts it. The "dance" is living on the Earth plane and living in the spiritual World. Oh, how I love the spiritual World. It is like an unquenchable thirst and it never ends. I love meditating with my Angels. They are so much fun! They dance with me. And I love to dance. I couldn't dance for quite a while when I was sick.

God's Ironic Satire

This is how my life was going: something came to me in my mind or I saw something and then it had a major significance in my life.

One day I had been talking to Monya for quite a while about many different things. I had been struggling with all that has happened to me. What came to me at the end of our conversation is that I just need to surrender to God and all things will fall into place. I was struggling with the path of becoming a medium. From what I remember reading in the Bible, this was not something I should do; although, there were seers in the Bible and dream interpreters. I had to wrestle with this. It seemed like these gifts were just given to me without me asking for them. It all just came to me as one thing led to another while I healed.

The next day, I was outside talking to God. I said to Him, "I need to know if this is truly okay with you." I was talking through this whole process of how I had gotten sick and what became my path to healing. This helped increase the vibration of my being and one thing just led to another. I knew the God of the Universe knew all of this already, but I needed to talk it all out from the beginning to end. I needed to make sense of it all. This is what our egos try to do: make sense of everything. As I finally got to the end of what I was relating, I just said, "Well, I guess I am never going to know whether you want me to do this or not, but I look at things this way: if St. Bernadette in Lourdes, France, never said anything about the Immaculate Conception coming to her 18 times, then millions of people who go there would not be getting healed." This is the example I used to make sense of all this. Why do I use this example of the Immaculate Conception? The answer was something I was soon going to learn. There are no coincidences, just synchronicities. I couldn't explain what was happening and I couldn't deny it, either. I simply said, "I am just going to surrender to this." Bingo! I took maybe two steps, looked down, and right there were two huge mourning dove feathers. I hadn't received feathers in a long time. I was elated! It was as if a light went on in my brain. Just surrender to it! This was my answer!!

I spoke to Monya and asked her what mourning dove feathers meant; she has told me in the past that the specific animals, birds and feathers that come to you are significant. It is the Universe speaking to us through them. Monya's text to me of what it meant was this:

haahahahahahahahahaahaaha OMG!!!!!!! LOL!!!!!!! So

Happy for you!!! Wait til you read this!!!! LOL!!!!

This was the next part of the text message:

The Mourning Dove means you are receiving true divine guidance through your feelings and intuition. Trust it.

The night before this happened the word "satire" came to me from nowhere. It came to me again in my sleep, so often that night, that it woke me up until I wrote it down. I told Monya I didn't know what it meant, but I had heard the word before but didn't remember what the definition of the word is. She texted me back saying:

You are killing me Angela!!!!!!!!!!!!!!!!! This is GREAT!!! There's your irony satire. Just surrender, you don't need to go through the whole song and dance. God has a great sense of humor.

Holy Feathers and Sage

Holy Sage From the Thin Air

THE NEXT MORNING I was purifying myself with burning sage as I have done every morning since meeting Monya. Saging yourself is one of the most sacred rituals that goes back thousands of years, as it is used to purify. Gary was in the room with me and as I was saging myself, clearing my aura, and acknowledging the fear of all of this as this is what Monya has taught me to do; she says to just acknowledge the fear. Fear can either stop us from living or it can be a teacher and will have no hold on us. As I was doing this, something came off the end of the sage leaf. It looked like an ash from the burned sage, as this happens frequently. I reached my hand out and I was saying to Gary, "Wow, that looks just like a feather!" We both said "No, that has to be an ash." I looked down in my hand ... and we each paused, smiled, and just looked at each other. Yes, it was a feather! It just appeared out of thin air! Weirder things have happened I am sure, but this came out of nowhere; we both saw it and it wasn't burned. I still have it. I keep them all. I have probably 50 feathers by now!

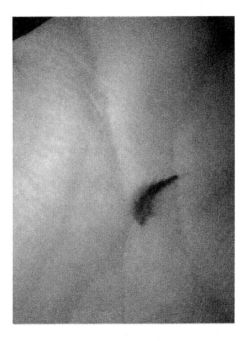

Holy Ash

There is a man who Wayne Dyer talked about in one of videos, whose name is Sai Baba. Sai Baba was a holy man and experienced holy ash just appearing out of nowhere. He could just pull it out of the air. This was his reality. Why did this happen? Was it just because of his belief that it could? I am not sure, but he was asked this question in an interview one day: "So, you think you are God?" And Sai just looked at the interviewer and said, "Yes, I am ... and so are you. The only difference between us is that I believe this and you doubt it." The reporter did not say much after that.

Finding Feathers in Strange Places

There is a room upstairs in my house that we decided to clean out and make into my healing room. We call this our Sacred Room. This room was an attic space full of boxes, seasonal decorations, and just a lot of things you would put into this kind of spare room. We basically used it for a "catch all" room. Gary, Zachary, Zachary's friend Alberto, and I were cleaning it out one day. We started to move some boxes and underneath were picture frames. There were several picture frames in a pile; one frame displayed a poem that Gary had written for me about 15 years ago. It was poem about me being an Angel here. It was amazing to read it again after so many years, after having gone through what I have been experiencing with the Angels; but what was most incredible about this picture frame was that there were about 8 black skinny feathers, about an inch to an inch and half long inside the frame! These were not there when Gary wrote the poem for me. They were not in any of the other picture frames, just this one. I have these pictures, also. We all saw this. What we saw was absolutely amazing to all of us! Zachary and Alberto were astonished that the feathers were in it, but they really didn't understand the way Gary and I understood. We all just looked at each other completely shocked.

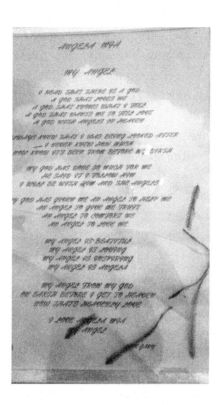

The night following the sacred room adventure, Gary, Cody, and I were in the room just talking. I was sitting on the floor, having a cup of tea, and Gary was standing next to me and he was looking at the air, rather peculiarly. He put his hand out in a cup like fashion and caught a very small white feather. Then more of them started to just "fall" from the ceiling. We were watching them fall and catching them in our hands! We all saw this and were catching them in awe. There was no physical explanation for this. It was just happening.

I was beginning to finally believe that all of what I was experiencing, hearing, and learning, had some merit.

Sometimes, God has to hit you over the head with a hammer many times to get you to pay attention. I had many, many beautiful, loving bumps on my head. Check your head, you probably do, too.

You Get Back What You Give

Positive Words and Thinking

As TIME WENT ON, I kept experiencing written words in my head. I saw the words Love, Light, Joy, Peace, Kindness, Goodness, etc. These words continued one after another. I saw them as small words growing bigger and bigger until they were just too big for my brain and then the image would "pop"; then the next word would come and the same thing happened. It was a trip to say the least, but this is what I was experiencing. I looked at people and had compassion for them instead of getting mad, upset, or frustrated. The things that had happened to me in my past started to not matter anymore. The money that people owed us didn't matter anymore. What mattered was their happiness. These people who did these things were used as an instrument to make me aware of what I needed to re-

 lease. We need to release all things within us that are not

love, as this is all we are. The Universe will continue to give you challenging situations in your life until you learn the lesson and let it go.

We have been programmed to fight for what we want to happen. There is so much that is wrong with this Planet right now. Both God and Mother Mary have told me this. There is so much to do to fix it, but we can't fix it by focusing on the negative and what we don't want to happen; we fix it with what we do want to happen. Do you want peace on the Planet? Practice spreading peace. Do you want forgiveness? Practice forgiving others. Do you want happiness? Practice spreading happiness. These are just a few of the many actions you can take to change this Planet. All of what you give out comes back to you. This World is a mirror to your life. There is a collective consciousness on Earth. This collective consciousness is from all of us and all our thoughts. Can you imagine, if we all started spreading love and light to everyone and everything, what a World this would turn into? I can guarantee that money and having material things would not be what people would be craving. Try it in your own life. Focus on what you do want with a pure heart and focused intention, and you will see things change; I guarantee it will not be about money.

More of the Angels

Drawing the Angels

My journey continued and at this point, as I listened to all the authors on Hay House radio, I started to draw. At first it was just a type of filigree design. It was a type of flow design that I just couldn't stop drawing. If I didn't have paper handy I would grab a napkin or anything else that was around that I could draw on. I needed to keep drawing this same design. It was a flow. It was as though it was just oozing out of me, for lack of a better word. This lasted for a week or so, and then I started to draw Angels. Certainly in the past I had been inclined to doodle every now and then, but nothing similar to what I was drawing now. I now have at least 40 different pictures of Angels. They are all different. In the past I had a hard time finishing anything. But each time I drew an Angel, I needed to finish it, and then it was time to draw the next one. The Angels were

FROM SICK TO BLISS TO CONVERSATIONS WITH GOD
Angela Mia White
96

telling me that they want people to know that they are here, and that we are never alone. That is what I am trying to do.

In my first meeting with Monya, I showed her the pictures of the filigree as well as all the Angels that I had drawn up until that day. She was so amazed that it took her breath away. She told me she has never seen anything like this. She was thinking that I may have been channeling people who had passed. That was a lot for me to comprehend. All this was completely new to me, but I loved that she loved the drawings. Could I really do all of this? I was realizing that I was entering a place in my soul where it was talking to me and I needed to listen.

The Angels kept talking, I kept listening, and writing down all that they said. I love them all. Arch Angel Michael is with me all the time. He is my protector and Arch Angel Raphael is with me to help me heal. He is a healing Angel. Arch Angel Chamuel is the Angel of Love and self-love. Arch Angel Metatron is the leader of all of them and he is with me constantly to make sure this book gets sent to the World. There are more of them. I don't have any hold on them, either. They have explained to me that they are a type of essence as we can understand it here on Earth. The Angels can be with everyone all the time; we just have to ask for their help. They only will interfere in life, without us asking, if we are in a situation that is life threatening to us and we are not supposed to die. Angels are God's messengers. They let us know what He wants us to know. There have been several sightings of the Angels and there will be several more as I am told. This is truly the Age of Aquarius.

Channeling the Angels

One day I was typing an email to Monya; the message was from me to Monya in the beginning, then all of a sudden it wasn't from me anymore. There was a huge surge of light and love coming through me to get into this email for Monya. I started to type the words that I was hearing to write down. It was almost like a knowing of what I was to write. The Angels were starting to write through me, and they had message for Monya. I really didn't know how to handle this. What I did was that I typed what they wanted me to write, and then I typed my own message in a separate email. I explained the email situation to Monya and asked her if she wanted to see it. She said, "If it is a message from the Heavens I need to see it." I said okay, and sent her both of the emails. She told me that it made perfect sense to her. This happened again right after Monya's email. The next letter was for my mother. I was told not to give it to her yet, though; I was told that I would know when it was the right time. I agreed to this. I don't argue with what the Angels ask me to do, as I know they always know what is best.

Big Happenings

This Is Big

AT THIS POINT I was learning at light speed it seemed. I was continually having more and more synchronicities and more and more was making sense to me. As much as I loved what was happening, I fought it for a long time. I fought against my own soul. I was completely programmed to believe that I should not go outside the box. I believed that I needed to stay just where I was and that I shouldn't move in any direction that was unknown to me. This is fear-based thinking. I lived like this for a while but the message started to get bigger than I was, it was getting bigger than any religion, even my Christian faith. The message I received is big. One of the many things I have been told is that I am here to be a channel of love and light. I came to realize that this is what WE ALL ARE in essence. We are love and light. Most people don't realize that we are not our bodies, or our minds. We are so much more! Our consciousness is not confined to our minds in our heads; it goes out to the Universe whether we like it or not. We have so much power that is suppressed by fear. Because it's either fear or love we come from. Every thought you think is coming from either love or fear. Break down every thought you have by questioning the reason behind the thought, and before you know it, you will see where it originates. For example, I ask myself, "Are people going to think I am weird and crazy when this book comes out?" Well, why do I think I am asking myself that question? The answer is, "Because I am afraid of not being loved anymore." You see? The thought is based in fear. Alternatively, a thought coming from love is, "I am okay with what people think of me after this book is out in the World. If they don't understand right now they aren't meant to and if they ridicule me, it is just from their own fear of not understanding. I love them for being who they are." See the difference? I am choosing to think out of love rather than fear, and you can, too.

First channel of Mother Mary

How crazy does that sound? I am still learning to replace that word "crazy" with other words. Today, we will go with "beautiful." How beautiful does that sound? One day I was out on my back steps meditating. It was pretty cold outside, as it was winter, but I wanted to be outside. I feel very close to God when I am outside. Monya told me that she wanted me to meditate every day to get in touch with my spirit guides. As I was doing the meditation, it was not only the Angels who were there with me that day. There was someone different. This was someone who I had seen before in other meditations. Previously, I hadn't known who it was, but that day I finally realized it was Mother Mary! I asked Michael, "It's Mother Mary isn't it?" I felt a tingling all over my body every time I said her name. I immediately started crying. I knew this is why the "Let It Be" sayings were coming to me from everywhere. This is why I cried uncontrollably every time I heard the song. This is why I used St. Bernadette seeing Mother Mary at Lourdes of France as justification for all that was happening to me. This was her and she was coming to me. This was all overwhelming and wonderful all at the same time. I was learning that this was all real, even though it was not on this Earth plane and it was hard to explain to people; but this is real.

Meditations and Manifesting

That night I still had a hard time grasping that Mother Mary wanted to give me messages, so I wanted to see if other people were experiencing this, too. It was very hard for me to tell my family about Mary coming to me, but I told Gary and Zachary who were in the room at the time. In the evening, I searched the Internet to find any example of others channeling Mother Mary and on the website page was a picture of the same person that I had seen during my meditation! It was the same person. It was Mother Mary! In my prior meditations, I had written down the description of how she looked. This was her! How do you handle something like this? Well, I totally did not know how to handle it and said, "Oh my God!" several times; I had my hand over my mouth while looking at the computer. My eyes were like saucers as I gazed at this image that I had seen earlier in my meditation. Cody, my youngest son, was across from me; he is pretty receptive and highly sensitive like me. He actually thought someone must have died, based on the way I was looking at this picture. That is how distraught I looked. I tried to tell them what I had just experienced and I was crying and kind of hyperventilating. Gary and all of my children, and also my son Zachary's girlfriend, Laura, were there to witness all this. I am not making any of this up; it really happened, and she really had messages for me. I will put one in this book, but please don't mock her.

One night I was practicing Kundalini Yoga. This is a yoga practice that I swear helps you get connected to your God on a much deeper level. Probably three quarters of the way through the session, I felt this presence tell me to just "let go"; I was to simply allow the things that were happening to me to happen without judgment. This was a pretty strong message and it came to me over and over again, often enough that I knew I needed to listen. I had never thought I would ever hear God. As I was hearing this message, I focused on heeding the message through the remainder of my yoga session. Then I went to take a bath. I went into the bathroom and as I was talking to the Angels as I do every night, Mother Mary was there and she appeared to me on the wall. I was amazed that she appeared to me only in an outline form, but I knew it was Her. I needed to remember where she was on the wall so I got a pencil and drew the outline that I saw. That night the message that she gave to me was pretty strong. She sounded almost peeved. She was upset about the Planet and how things are going here. I would not have imagined that Mother Mary could get mad or ever talk about the Planet in a critical way, but this message was not happy. She is our Mother and cares about all of us. This is what she said:

Good Evening, Blessed Ones,

I hope you are all living life to its fullest potential as that is what life has been created for.

Please do not fear. Fear will keep you from attaining what you were brought here to do. I have been seeing the wretchedness of the Planet. God designed this Planet for harmony and peace and man has been disrupting the tranquility. I am sorry to be so upset but I see the turmoil in families: the murders, the gunshots, the deaths that have been caused by other people's lack of self-respect. I am praying for this Planet every day and I wish for you to join me in this. I need your positive spirit and energy to be lifting each other up in unity. Please understand that I know some of you are not aware of what you are doing to each other; that is why I need the ones who are awake to help me. Please keep posting positive items on social media. Do anything you can to get them to stop, and wake up. I am sorry that I am upset at the moment, but it is so unnecessary. Go back to the simple things in life. I know most people will not heed this message, but you need to do the best you can, Angela, to help them see. We know you can do this for us. You have been chosen to do this. We are just helping you remember. Please come to us for guidance and reassurance that you are doing the right thing. I am just like you. I am spirit and was in human form. I am still here guiding people, praying for people, loving people. Please *help them see how loved they are and how worthy they are of that love. Make sure you post everything we tell you to. Tell Gary this is what we say. This is real. We don't know how else to let you know. God wants you to love people unconditionally. Keep trying to do this; you are doing great. We know you don't like the news and hearing bad things from people. But this is what we need you to do. The bad stuff in people is necessary for their hearts. Gary is a wonderful man and was chosen for you to endure everything you did. Don't worry, he can handle a lot. He is here for you and so are we. Please ask us anything you want or need. Get some rest tonight.*

We are filled with love for you and the World.

Gratitude and Blessings to you,

Mother Mary

This was a lot for me to handle. I looked up on the Internet whether anyone who channels Mother Mary had experienced her anger. I thought she was just about roses and sweet thoughts. This is not the case. She is our mother and she is not happy with what is happening on the Earth. This is another reason I am to write this book. She wants people to wake up. As I was searching for the answer on the Internet, I did not have to go very far. The first picture that I saw was an image of whom and what I had drawn on my bathroom wall. My drawing was the same as the picture on the Internet. In relaying some of this information to my dad, I told him that Mother Mary gets mad. I asked him if he knew this and he said to me, "She sure does!" He gave me a book that was about an inch-and-a-half thick that a priest had channeled from her. Talking to my dad about what I had experienced from her helped me tremendously. Finding out that I am not the only one this happens to when I put my hands on a keyboard was quite comforting.

Just so you understand this about Mother Mary, she does not represent any particular religion. She represents love, just as Jesus, Buddha, the Dalai Lama, Mother Teresa, St. Francis, and many, many others do. This is what their whole journeys were about. This is what my journey is for. This is what your journey is for. Wake up to love. This is your soul.

We Are Love and Light

Bliss Is Who I Am

ONE OF THE WORDS I hear frequently from people who are awakening to all that is, is "bliss." This life to me is "bliss." I feel it is part of who I am. If I could rename myself it would be, Angela Mia "Bliss" White! This life has been referred to as a ride and what a ride it is. I am so blessed to know that I am a channel of love and light on this Planet to help people heal as we are, the Divine. It is "bliss" to be able to help people. I listen to music all the time and I can't help but dance. It doesn't matter where I am, my soul feels it and my body just flows to it. I probably embarrass my kids when I am with them, but I can't stop it. I also hug people all the time. It is a strange feeling when I can't do this. Hugging fills my heart with more love and light. Hugs are very important for survival for everyone! It is food for my soul! All the kids who come to our house know that they are going to get hugs when they arrive. The Angels tell me that when we hug someone, the Angels hug us back, both of us at the same time. Isn't that so beautiful? They are thrilled when love is spread. Please do this. Hug people. They need it. Our World needs it.

I have read that the heart has an electromagnetic field that is 60 times larger than the electromagnetic field of the brain. When you are feeling love and appreciation in your heart, your heartbeat stabilizes and this energy can heal your entire body. I can attest to this. I was told one night to hug my own body and tell it that I love it. Hug your shoulders and say "I Love you, shoulders." Hug your legs and say, "I love you, legs." They wanted me to do this to my whole body until my whole body was covered in love. I felt strange doing this, but it was absolutely amazing how I felt after I had done it. I continue to do this today. Love is here for us for many reasons, but it is definitely here for us to heal.

I was out in the yard the other day and I was looking at all of nature around me. I was realizing that we don't have to be anything to be loved. We need to do things in this life to get by to live, but you don't have to BE anything or any-one in order to be loved. You were loved before you were even a thought in your parents' minds. You have been loved forever. I hope you are getting this. It is something that we all have to come to grips with. It is still difficult for me to understand and accept that I am loved in this manner.

I was driving to my friend Marcia's house the other day, and as I was looking at the birds flying in the sky, and the trees and people in cars, the song from the "Doobie Brothers" came on called *Here to Love You*. This is what God, the Universe, Source is saying to us. Everything is "here to love you." Yes, *you!* You are loved. This whole Planet screams, "I love you!" and I get to awaken to this every day. When you can look at weeds and realize that they are not "choking out" the other plants and understand instead that they are "loving and hugging" the other plants, you tend to see life in a very different way. There are thousands of us on this Planet right now who are awakening to all this and we all tend to say the same thing: we are love, and we are one. There is no separation between us and God, as we are Him.

First Call of Laying on of Hands

Monya was having a gentleman friend stay with her for a little while; while he was there, I felt there were messages coming in for Monya so I "tuned in," so to speak. There was in fact a message, and it included me. Now, I was feeling pretty weird about this message, because this woman had taught me so much; she is my teacher, friend, mentor, guide, and so much more. I have been blessed to know her, and here I was, getting a message that I was to go and lay my hands on this gentleman. I was told that I would be taught what to do and where to place my hands on him so that healing could enter him. I was also told that Monya should ask me again, as she had done before, if there were any more messages that had come in for this gentleman. All this information was in the first message. I told Monya I felt pretty weird sending this message to her as it included me, but it wasn't for me—it was for him, so I sent it. Monya was thrilled that I was asked to do this. This was the first healing that I was asked by my guides to do.

This is how they prepared me for the healing. I had gone to Monya's to meet this man prior to the healing and what a meeting it was. I immediately saw his spirit. It was beautiful and I told him that. I explained what I had been instructed to have him do. I was told that he should bathe in sea saltwater and wear white. He did not have anything white with him, so I brought him one of Gary's T-shirts. I was also told that he should do the Ho'oponopono mantra before he goes to sleep. He did these things on Friday and I came to see him on Sunday. John of God also has those who come to see him wear white while he heals them. I explained to him what I was going to do, which was nothing. I was going to lay my hands on him where I was told to and God and the Angels would do all the work. I told him how humbled I was and what an honor it was to help him. Please do not think that God is unreachable. He is always there and waiting for you to call on Him. Look inside yourself and you will find Him. Monya stays in close contact with this gentleman, and says he is doing wonderfully.

I have realized that God wants me to be here for people, to let them know how much they are loved. Deeply, deeply loved. He needs us to get in touch with our own souls. Our souls need to accept and embrace all of who we are. We need to accept our good and bad parts; then we will be whole.

Who Am I? I Am Love, and So Are You

It is February, 2014. I went to see Dr. Arora again. I am so blessed to be her patient. It was wonderful to see her. As soon as I walked into her office, I asked if I could give her a hug. She said, "Of course." I then asked her if she wanted to go over the results for my thyroid testing or talk first. She said, "Let's talk first." I started talking about what has happened in my life since the last time I saw her. I know I said earlier that I don't have the gift of gab, but I was so full of what I needed to tell her within a small allotment of time, that I was explaining too fast, and I needed to slow down and catch my breath, literally. She went out to get both Gary and me some water. She came back into the office and I continued to tell her that I have been told many things. I have been told that "I am here for many, many people and that I am a catalyst for many." So I looked into her eyes and asked her what she was thinking and she just paused and said with tears in her eyes, "I believe that you are here for me!" She just kind of looked at me with that stare. I get this stare a lot now. People just look into my eyes and they see something. Something that is hard to describe. I believe they see the love of the Divine. I believe that I can help them look into their own soul and get to that place where they have separated themselves from themselves. I am here to hold that love for them. I am an empty channel and I am filled with love and light. She saw this. She started to cry, as she exclaimed, "Who are you?" She is on her journey of awakening. She saw the love and light in my eyes and I saw it in hers. I just said, "It's okay, I am here for you, too." I am here to show people who they really are. You really are love and light and as you awaken you will   realize this. You will realize who you really are. Gary was sitting in the office with me and witnessed the whole conversation.

I am here for many people as they become more and more awake. Dr. Arora and I started to develop a reciprocal relationship. It was a wonderful feeling that she was seeing in my eyes what I have been designed to do here on Earth. We did eventually discuss my test results: my blood pressure was a healthy 120/80 and I have no thyroid issues! I AM Healthy, I AM Happy, I AM Holy. I learned to say this every day from James Van Praagh. He liked to say, "Happy am I, Healthy am I, Holy am I." I start the phrase with I AM as that is who we are. We are the great I AM.

Blue Rays

As I am led to more and more gifts, I am being led to know about Blue Rays. Blue Rays have chosen to come to Earth to raise the consciousness of the Planet and fill it with love. Blue Rays are bearers of Christ Consciousness; not just Christ consciousness, but also the understanding that we are one—not just with other people, but we are one with everything on this Planet and the Universe. This is the second coming of Christ. It is still hard for me to comprehend this, as I have not been programmed to think this way. It is the awakening that a lot of us are experiencing, as we come to understand that we are the same God that made this whole Universe. We are God. We are love. We are light.

I will tell you how Blue Rays have entered my life. I was at Body, Mind, and Spine, which is my chiropractor's office. I go there two days a week for spine manipulation to aid in my healing. This place is a place of healing and is becoming a spiritual portal for people. I was waiting in the reception area for Dr. Faith to talk with me about my progression. There are many, many books there in the office. I said to myself, "Okay, I know there is a book here that I am supposed to see," and there it was—a book called *Soul Psychology*. I didn't know the author, but the picture on the front of the book included Mother Mary, the Dalai Lama, Jesus, and more. It also had bright golden light rays shining on the picture of all these people. I said, "That is it." It was known to me because I had drawn this "light" before. I brought the book home and I looked up the author thinking that maybe this person's publishing company could tell me how to publish my book. I knew this book was going to get published I just didn't know how it was going to happen. So I thought I would help this process by looking up the publishing company that Joshua David Stone, Ph.D., used to publish his book. I looked up Light Technology Publishing. I had hit the mother lode. This company published books about the awakening process: from Angels to UFOs to Blue Rays. The website was asking me if I was a Blue Ray. I saw words like indigos, enlighten, and Shekinah (which means "language of light" in Hebrew). Though I will not explain in this book why these words have significance to me, they all do. I started to read on the website about the Blue Rays, and though I still need to read more, I read on the site about the second coming of Christ and those who have come to Christ Consciousness. It immediately struck me, because that morning as I had done a healing on my son Zachary, there was a blue light in my hallway.

This Is the Age of Aquarius

This Is the Age of Awakening

A FEW WEEKS before reading about the Blue Rays, I watched *Wake Up*. This film helped me immensely. It gave me validation of what was happening to me, and indeed what was happening to other people. A young man named Jonas Elrod one day, out of the blue, just started seeing spirits, auras, people who have passed over, shapes, etc. He was going through his awakening process. He went around the World to talk with people who had expertise in these experiences. One place he went was a mystery school run by a woman named J.Z. Knight. This place was amazing. They taught about the brain and how it works in the spiritual realm and here on Earth. This school was intriguing to me, so I looked it up on YouTube. I found out that Ms. Knight channels a person called Ramtha. I have no idea who Ramtha is, but Ms. Knight was channeling people the way I do, so I researched more about her. There was a video on YouTube of her appearing on a Merv Griffin show. The guest appearance had taken place probably 35 years ago. Merv was asking her questions and one of the questions was about Jesus coming back. As I listened, I was given information about what she was going to say before she said it. She said it wasn't that Jesus was coming back in physical form; it was that the Planet was going to awaken to the understanding that we are God.

Jesus said you will do greater things than I. That's just how God is. He wants us to each have such wonderful experiences here on Earth. I went through hell to get Heaven on Earth and I never want to leave this place of love, light, and synchronicities. This is truly the love of God that I am experiencing through everything in my life. I feel like King Midas, in that everything I touch turns to gold. Not because of me in the flesh, but because of Him who is me, in my soul.

Me? God's Scribe?

By this time, I had been hearing from the Angels and Mother Mary. This is amazing in itself. Then one day I woke up and went on Facebook and I saw a man named Neal Donald Walsch. The caption under his picture was "God's scribe." This sounded like what was happening to me. I had no idea who Neale Donald Walsch was. I started listening to his video and realized that what he was experiencing was the same thing that I was experiencing. It turns out that he is the man that wrote *Conversations With God*. That same morning, the tree in my backyard was calling to me.

Yes, you read correctly, the tree was calling to me. It was God. He asked me to go out to the tree to have a conversation with Him. (This tree, I had told Monya a few weeks prior to this day, had many spirits in it. I knew there were many spirits there. I could feel them.) The same morning that I read about Neal being God's scribe, I said to Gary, "You love me, right?" He looked at me funny and said, "Yes, of course. What's wrong?" I told him that the tree was calling to me and it was God and that I needed to go to the tree to have a conversation with Him. I said, "Am I crazy?" He said, "Ang, people that are crazy don't ask 'Am I crazy?' No, you are not crazy, I love you, dress warmly." It was below zero that day and very windy. I hate the cold weather and I am not one to go out on such a day, but it was God. You don't say no, even if you are cold. I dressed warmly and went to the tree. There was much snow, probably over a foot or so, but I managed. I took a pen and notebook with me and had a conversation with Him. The first thing He did was tell me where to sit so that I would be shielded from the wind. This is how He is. I asked several questions and received several answers. Some pointed questions were so personal that I will not include them; but I will share the general questions and answers with you. Once you learn who you really are, you will be able to do this, too.

This is what I have been told:

I was called to the tree with many spirits.
He told me where to sit so I would be blocked from the wind as it was below zero outside and very windy.
He said, 'This is your burning bush.'

I asked, 'Why Me?'

He answered, 'I am like Moses, I will be bringing many people to the light. The light of knowing. [This is why I was so attached to Moses as a child and adult.] I am being rebirthed to the light.'

I asked, 'How do I explain this?'

He said, 'They have to have faith, not just in me who is you, but in themselves and everything else in their life.'

I asked, 'What is the meaning of life?'

He said, 'I have given you life to live to the fullest. You know what it is. It is different for everyone.'

I asked, 'How is it that I hear you?'

He said, 'Because you listen, you have faith, you have much love in your heart to give.'

I asked, 'I'm not crazy?'

He said, 'Listen to Gary. I have given him much wisdom. I will let you know who it is you need to talk to. Monya is one of them, there are many more.'

I asked, 'Who am I in my soul?'

He said, 'You are love and light, you are wisdom and peace. You are Sun and Moon. You are everything I have made and more. You are a blessed being as is everyone else.'

He continued, 'You were right in saying that there are many spirits here. They are everywhere. They are in you and in everyone else.'

'Thank you for being my voice.'

[I was crying after hearing this]

'It is all right, Angela, you were designed for this. You can handle the ridicule; it is not that, it is just their disbelief.'

I asked, 'What do I tell people of different religions?'

He said, 'Tell them I love them all deeply. They can get stuck in their religion and understanding. When they are stuck in their beliefs and thinking, they can't flow. I am flow. They need more of this flow in their lives.'

'Tell the people in your life that I talk, they need only to just sit and listen and believe.'

'I am in you, you are me.'

I asked, 'How does this work that I am you and you are me?'

He said, 'Please listen; you are so blessed to know these things you need to teach this.'

'This Planet is in tough shape. I need you Angela.'

'Please know that you are my vessel and it doesn't matter who believes or who doesn't. You are the seed to plant this understanding.'

I asked, 'Are you going to call me here again?'

He said, 'Yes, many times.'

I asked, 'Have you called me here before?'

He said, 'Yes, many times.'

I said, 'You know I don't like the cold.'

He said, 'It shows how much you are listening. It's not about obeying; it is about understanding it. Please let this penetrate your soul.'

'Your soul is in me. I am in you. Jesus is my son and I love you just like I love Him; just like you love Zachary, Anthony, and Cody.'

I asked, 'How are they going to handle all of this, that I am having a conversation with God?'

He said, 'I have done this forever with people. It should be accepted by now, but they will be fine. They will be confused, but it's for them that you are doing this. This is to better the Planet and in turn better the people. All the saints are your guides; yes, Mother Mary, also.'

I asked, 'Why did Jesus have to die like that?'

He said, 'Jesus did that to show how much you need to love

me, which is the same as loving you! How much I love you, who is you! He did not die as depicted.'

I asked, 'How do I explain this?'

He said, 'You don't explain, just love.'

'They will see, they will see, they will see, they will see, they will see, they will see, they will see.'

'I am.'

I know what you are thinking. The same thing I was. Did I really have a conversation with God? I really did have a conversation with God.

I have been to this tree many times. Each time I go, I bring my questions and get my answers. One day, as I was walking up the hill, I was listening to songs on my phone. As I walked, the song switched all by itself to the song *Tupelo Honey*, by Van Morrison. Van is someone I listen to frequently. This particular day I wasn't listening to Van. In this song there is a verse that says over and over again, "She's an Angel." That was all I needed to hear.

It Was Time for a Lot to Happen

Telling Mom about Her Letter

ONE DAY I WAS talking on the phone to my mom and was explaining all that had been happening to me. The last thing that I had told her prior to this call was that I had been hearing the Angels. She knew nothing about what had happened since then, so I started telling her everything. I didn't hold back anything. I was on my way home and was just about done bringing her up to date when I drove by a field near my house. As I looked over, I saw a wall of light with sparkles in it. I could see right through it. It looked as though it was a type of heat or smoke coming out of the ground in one area, and about 20 feet away from it there was a goldish hue. Like royalty was there. I wish I could print from memory what it looked like. I immediately knew that this was an Angel! I was screaming and crying on the phone. I told her that I needed to turn around, that I was seeing Angels in the field. I went back and pulled into the store near there. I got out of my car and ran to the field. It was the middle of winter and this field had about a foot and a half of snow on it. I didn't care. I ran up the street and ran into the field. They were still there! As I ran toward them they faded. I saw a brilliant gold light in the tree. It was probably one-third the size of the tree. I was yelling, "I see you! I see you!" I did not handle it well. They told me that they would not show themselves to me until I could handle it better. I am not sure I will ever be able to handle this. I hope I will, but I don't know. I was recently speaking with Mother Mary and she told me it had been Her and the Angels. She comes with the Angels and the Angels come with Her. She told me that she would allow me to see her again with Gary, when I can handle it better. I am waiting patiently for that day to come. There is a woman named Emma who gets gold dust on her face when she sees Mother Mary (I found this out about Emma after I saw what I saw in the field that day).

It was about at this time that I realized the time had come to let my mom know that I had a message for her from the Angels. I told her that I had received it a while ago, but when it had come was not the right time to share it; now was definitely the right time to share it with her. I went home and shared the letter with her. I also shared the first letter describing my conversation with God. She was amazed to say the least, but also, she was frightened for me, thinking that I could receive negative backlash when this is made public. I just hope that people understand that they, too, are capable of having all these experiences. Who doesn't want Heaven on Earth?

I have had many communications with Mother Mary and God and now just today I spoke to Jesus. Other people have done this and continue to do this. I am not the only one. There is actually a book called, *Teach Only Love from the Course in Miracles*. I have yet to read this book, but I have been told that the book was channeled from Jesus. It is all about Love. I saw something in my Sacred Room today. What I saw was the same vision I saw in the field but much, much smaller. I handled it much better. While doing my meditations, Mother Mary has often been there, and She finally brought me to see Her son, Jesus. I was so honored that She brought me to Him. After my meditation, I got to speak with Her again. While speaking with Her, I noticed that something was different. She was different. I asked who it was that I was speaking with and what I heard was, "This is Jesus." I cried, and felt honored, joyful, elated, and humbled that I would be speaking with Jesus. It was a three-page letter, but here is His message to people:

'What would you like people to know?' I want them to know that they are so loved that I died for them to know themselves. I want them to know that they are so loved and wanted and willed to be here. I want them to know that they all have a specific purpose and inside of them is where they will find the answer to that. I want them to know that they are a jewel in my crown. I want them to know that the nature that they see outside is in all of them. They are the birds and the fish and the plants and the stones and the water and the snowflakes and the grass and the trees. When they hurt the Earth they are hurting themselves. They are that and more. I want them to know that we are all one. WE ARE ALL ONE. I want them to know that the fighting amongst themselves needs to stop.

IT NEEDS TO STOP. Please send this message to all. I want them to be grateful for what they do have and not covet others' gifts. They are not missing anything. Each is to have what they have according to themselves.

Wow. Yes. Wow. Sometimes, there are just no words I can use to describe this. It never gets old. Now the task is to get people to heed what all the guides are trying to help us understand. I believe that now is the time. It is the time of awakening.

"Believe" Is My Word and My Work

I had started to realize more clearly that everything I have gone through is an awakening process, just as Monya told me. I wasn't just hearing it from her any longer; I was finally believing it. "Believe" is my word now. One day I wrote down two words on which I often confuse the spelling. These two words are" definitely" and "believe." When I checked my notes app on my iPhone, to once again verify the spelling of "believe," the page said "Definitely Believe." I am definitely believing. I love how the Divine works! One of the things I have learned from Wayne Dyer is that, "We are not humans having a spiritual experience, we are spirits having a human experience." I am starting to understand this statement. Just a side note: the quote from Wayne appears on Monya's business card, and was there long before she met me; another synchronicity.

The "believe" word comes up everywhere. A bracelet that I wear every day has "believe" on it. I have seen this word several times in this spiritual walk. The Angels and other guides ask me to do things and back up the requests with synchronicities that I just can't deny. I was asked by my guides to present Monya a gift for her continued healing. Monya is my lifeline, teacher, mentor, and friend, and I was asked to do this for her. I felt strange doing this, as she had been walking the spiritual walk for 25 years, while mine has just begun. I am a newbie, but that doesn't matter. The guides were telling me that everyone needs healing no matter who they are. They asked me to present her with one of the two identical music boxes that I had acquired since the time my children were infants. Each plastic, windup music box plays *Somewhere Over the Rainbow*. The Wizard of Oz was significant to both Monya and me: it was the last movie that Monya watched with her son Scotty before his death, and it is the song I listened to as I nursed my children over the years. I found it odd that we both found significance in this song, but as time went on, I came to understand how the music box would help Monya continue healing from her devastating loss of Scotty. I kept hearing that I needed to present Monya with the music box. At first I ignored what I heard, but when I continued to hear it, I realized the importance of the message. A day later we went to my youngest son Cody's basketball game. We pulled into the parking lot of the school we thought was the location for the game. There on the window of the school was a flyer for a play that was going to be presented at the school. It was *The Wizard of Oz*. I said, "Okay, I get it. I will present it to her soon." We got to the correct school and on entering, what I saw on the whole wall took my breath away. The whole wall was a painting of *The Wizard of Oz*. Right next to it was the word,

"BELIEVE." I have pictures of this, also. I said, "Okay, okay, okay. I get it. I will present it to her." I went home and still did not do anything about the music box. That night the Oscars were on. We usually don't watch the Oscars, but it was what just happened to be on the TV. I was lying in bed and I saw Pink come out on stage and couldn't believe what I was hearing. I was completely amazed. If you saw the Oscars this year you know what she was singing. She was singing *Somewhere Over the Rainbow*! I was crying and Gary was asking me what was wrong. I proceeded to tell him what I was being asked to do. I went to my Sacred Room and asked Mother Mary to bless the music box and left it

there under the picture that I have of her. The next day I was speaking to Mother Mary and she asked if I remembered when she said to me, "No one knows loss like a mother losing a child." I said, "Yes." She told me that She wanted me to put that phrase on the card to Monya, wrap the music box in rainbow-colored paper and gift bag, and bring it to her. "But do not be there when she opens it," she told me. I said, "Okay, I can do this." I went to the store and got to the materials I needed as instructed, and went to Monya's house. I spoke with Monya about things that had been happening to me as I always do. She talked me through things as she always does, and then it was time for me to leave. As I was about to leave, she asked me a question about the gift I had given to her. I "asked" in my mind if I could stay and heard Mother Mary say, "Yes." I stayed with Monya and said to her, "Did you see the Oscars last night?" She immediately started to scream and cry and jump up and down. She doesn't watch the Oscars either, but she had been watching just like me, and she said, "When Dorothy said, 'There is no place like home.' I heard Scotty's voice say it and I knew he was home." Monya was healed from hearing his voice say this. I said, "Go open your gift." Again, tears of joy and healing flowed from Monya. Believe is my word, and now I remember how to spell it.

The House Blessing

I have been "called" to help other people heal. Monya was called to do a house blessing, as this particular house was not selling; the people who owned this home wanted to move to their new home, and no one was coming to see the house that was for sale. Monya was talking to God about this and she thought she heard that I was supposed to be a part of it. So she verified by asking God, "Does Angela need to be a part of this?" She turned on the radio and "Let It Be" was on the radio. She knew immediately that I needed to go with her to, what she thought, would be to learn. She asked me if I would like to accompany her and her friend Marcia to this house blessing. I said, "Yes, of course." I was very curious what a house blessing would be like, so I was happy to be invited. Prior to this, Monya had told me that if any message came in regarding this house blessing, to let her know about it. I didn't think anything would, as Monya was the one in charge of the house blessing. I did start getting information that something had happened to a child in the kitchen. There was healing needed for this child and then the house would sell. I received more information that I was going to need holy water for the kitchen, also. I gave Monya the information that I had received; she told me to come to her house and she would show me how she makes holy water. I went to her house and she showed me how to make it, I told her that I needed to bring it to the tree, the one where I talk to God, and leave the holy water there overnight. The weather was still extremely cold, but I did what I was asked to do. The following morning I went to the tree and the bottle of holy water was completely frozen. I was starting to panic, as Monya was supposed to pick me up soon. I started doubting that all this was supposed to have happened. I started to degrade myself and called myself "stupid." You should never talk to yourself like this. Everything you "mess up" is a learning experience. I came into the house and I was directed to go to my Sacred Room, turn on the electric fireplace, and place the bottle about 10 inches away from it. It was probably fewer than five minutes before the whole bottle was melted to all liquid. I started to feel better about everything and began to see that I needed to stop doubting myself and just believe. There is that word again: believe.

Monya picked me up and we drove to Marcia's house first to pick her up, as she was the one who had asked Monya to come do the house blessing. I had been in Marcia's house for about ten minutes; while sitting on the couch talking about the experiences that I had been hav-ing, I felt Mother Mary tell me that I needed to lay my hands on Marcia's husband's heart. I tried to "shrug" it away, as I had just met these people; but it was a pretty strong message. I started to cry as we were talking. Monya asked me why I was crying and I told her that I had been asked to place my hands on Mark's heart for him to receive healing from Mother Mary. She said, "Well, ask him if he minds if you do that." I asked Mark and he obliged. I pro-ceeded to lay my hands on his heart and tell him what Mother Mary was telling me to tell him. Marcia told us that he had recently had heart surgery. That was an interesting first meeting.

It was time to go to the house blessing. Monya, Marcia, and I drove to the house. When we arrived there was a woman who was sitting in the kitchen with the owners of the home. She was the mother of the woman who owned the house. This woman was just out of the hospital and was not supposed to be there. As we were all talking in the kitchen it came to me that the child who I had been told about, who had been hurt in the kitchen, was this grown woman. I looked at Monya and she looked at me and she said, "Do you understand?" I said, "Yes, I do." After the house blessing I went and spoke to this woman. I explained that I heal with Mother Mary and that I was there for her. She was the child in the kitchen who needed healing. We are all God's children. And Mother Mary is our Mother. The woman had that look that I get that says, "Who are you? Where did you come from?" She looked into my eyes and had that look of "Am I really that important that you came here for me?" She told me with tears in her eyes that she talks to Mother Mary every day. I was able to tell her that Mother Mary hears her and wants her to let go of all the past hurts in her life especially from her childhood. She told me that this is what she has been trying to do. She said thank you many times and said that she will continue to try to let go. This was simply amazing to me to learn that she talked to Mother Mary every day, and realized that because of the connection, I had been invited to go with Monya.

There has been several of that type of healings so far. I have also been asked to send people things for their continued healing. I was asked to send white roses to a woman named Peggy who just lost her husband, Steve; I had just met Peggy a couple weeks prior to this. I sent the white roses to her from Mother Mary. The woman emailed me and told me that the she and the funeral director wanted to have a flower that represented her husband's life and they had chosen white roses. I had no way of knowing this. Mother Mary did. I also received a few other validations for doing this.

It was my birthday a few weeks ago. My son Anthony told me that two of his friends, Mia and Heather, wanted to bring me a present for my birthday. I had not seen these friends of his for months but they were adamant about bringing me a present for my birthday. They walked through my door at 10 p.m. and gave me a dozen white roses! They had no idea of knowing either. I got back what I gave. The next morning I received another beautiful bouquet of flowers. These were from my son Anthony's friend, Austin. The flowers were beautiful, of course, and the message that came along with it was almost too much for me to take. This is what was written on a sheet of notebook paper from this 16-year-old boy: Happy Birthday Angela, I love you, From Austin. He drew a big heart underneath this. These kids are feeling the love that is from their own heart. This is what we are. We are love and they are all feeling it! I am teaching them how important it is to love themselves, and I am witnessing these changes in them.

Our Programming Needs Changing

I Am Sure There Will Be Naysayers;
I Was One of Them

I HAVE HAD TO come to terms with many things. I have had to strip everything down that I have been taught and programmed to believe. I did not think that any of this was possible. I have found that much of what I had been programmed to believe no longer makes sense to me. It doesn't support what has been happening in my life. I NEVER thought any of this was possible. People who know me and my story have seen me change into a completely different person from who I used to be.

To awaken to what I have been taught, I stripped down all that I was taught in my Christian religions and searched to understand where those beliefs had originated. When growing up, you are taught things you don't really ever think of questioning. I started questioning things. I was no longer just accepting what I had been taught my whole life. I stripped down all of my thoughts about the things that I believed. I took all of my feelings that came from all those beliefs and I was able to see clearly. I said to myself, "If I didn't know anything of my Christian faith, or the Bible for that matter, what would I be left with?" I would be left with people and Mother Nature and God. I would be left with the flowers, the stones, the animals, the plants, the herbs, the oils, the moon, the sun and the stars, the seasons, night, day, all of my experiences, and so much more! This is how people used to live. They lived off the land and they understood that an entity who is the Great Entity of All gave this to them. If your religion is teaching you to fear, you need to decide for yourself if you think that such a teaching is right.

We separate ourselves by our color, religion, sex, race, etc. We then are separated further with the borders of our properties and with where we live in different towns, cities, states, and countries. I know that these things have to take place in our World today. I'm using it as an illustration for you to see that the labels we put on ourselves are what separates us. If you took all those things away, you would see a bit more clearly. We see ourselves as a separate entity. We are not separate. We physically have separate bodies, but spiritually we are all part of each other. The more we stand in our own truth, and allow others to stand in theirs, the more we see that we are love and we are one.

I know that I have said this before, but it needs to be said again: we need to accept ourselves for who we are, including the good, the bad, and the ugly. It is all sacred. The bad and the ugly need to come out and be dealt with. The action of them coming to the surface will show you that you are out of balance; the old programming and hurts of the past are coming up to be released. Don't take it out on anyone else. Learn the lesson. Do the dance. Walk the walk. We are no better or no worse than anyone else. If you think you are better or worse you are just separating yourself. I know this is deep but if you think about it, it all makes complete sense. And by the way, as Carl Sagan made famous on the PBS series *Cosmos*, we are all made of the same stuff. We are stardust. How cool is that?

I Have Heard This Called "New Age Religion," but I Don't See It Like That

This Planet is definitely shifting into a different consciousness. A "peace" consciousness. I don't call my journey "New Age Religion." I don't call my journey any type of religion. If I had to call it anything, I would call it miraculous, beautiful, and loving signs from Heaven and Earth that has awakened me to all that is and all that may just be possible. I don't really think it needs a name, but some people call this "New Age." Apparently there are many articles that people have written on this "New Age" subject, as I have read many of them. In my opinion, based on what I have read, some of these articles are written by people who may have just "heard" what this is all about. It seems that they have formed their own opinion and then have written about what they think, is the definition of New Age based on the beliefs that were programmed into them. These articles are based in their own fear, which they then project onto others.

I assure you that if these articles were written by someone who receives feathers almost every day, who hears the Angels and the trees speaking to them, someone who has been awakened to all that is, who has been awakened to the fact that "we are love," the writing would be completely different. As I said before, you come from a place of love or fear. Love comes from the heart, fear comes from the mind. In my opinion some of these articles are written from people's own fears, from their own minds. It seems they are written with good intentions, with a desire to protect people from what the authors fear; but they are in fact boxing people in, as a result of what they have been programmed to believe. Some of these articles, in my opinion, were not written by someone who is actually experiencing their own awakening. If they were, the writing would be about love, peace, and healing.

My dad's church, not my dad, as his daughter has been going through all this, is against "New Age Religion." I'm sure many churches are, because they don't know what it is and are afraid of it. If they only knew that this awakening is to raise the vibration and consciousness of this incredible Planet to help people understand themselves, heal themselves, and bring peace. Have you ever heard Michael Jackson's song, *Heal the World*? I invite you to watch the video and listen to the words of this song. My husband and I went to a "Cirque du Soleil" performance that featured songs from Michael Jackson. As soon as I walked in, I knew that Michael knew the same truth that I now know. The stage had a curtain about 100 feet tall and 50 feet Wide, in the image of a tree. It could have been a picture of anything, but it was a tree and not just any tree, it was *my* tree.

Michael was a "lightworker." He was very misunderstood
and no one knows what really happened in his life except
him and the people directly involved. You can speculate
on what he did and didn't do if you like, but he was here
to wake us up to us being love. I am not saying he didn't
have problems (we all do), but he knew he was love and he
tried to wake up the World with his music that spoke of
love and awakening. This book is being written for the
same purpose. It is for you to wake up to You. You are love.

It seems as though people get caught up in what they
think this change of consciousness is. If they only could

wake up to see their own fear and think for themselves, this Planet would be much better off. Their fear is keeping them so stuck that they are going to miss it. If they only knew how at peace they would be by going inside of themselves and finding the Divine, they wouldn't be fighting so hard to keep people from finding this out for themselves. I know what this is all about and I have been chosen to tell you what it truly is. I also know others, who I have come in contact with from around the globe, who have been awakened to this consciousness; they, too, know what it is all about. We all can tell you what it is about. Ready? It is all about You; what comes from finding this out is love, peace and healing. We are one. Pretty simple concept, huh?

In the Sacred Room in my house, I have a statue of St. Francis because I love his heart that loved people and animals. I have a bust of Mother Mary that was presented to me by a new friend of mine, Dot Walsh, who was a big part of the Peace Abbey in Sherborn, Massachusetts. There have been many people who have visited the Peace Abbey to promote peace, including the Dalai Lama, Mother Teresa, and Muhammad Ali. What a priceless gift this is. I am extremely humbled to have such a precious artifact under my roof.

I have extreme reverence for all the Saints and Ascended Masters and I am grateful to all of them and for what they have brought to this World by teaching love and peace. This is my heart. I am grateful. I have extreme love in my heart that enables me to pray for people, love that I have never had before. I have a prayer board that I was directed to make and I have my family, relatives, friends, my children's friends, their families, and acquaintances on it.

There are also people on the board who I do not know personally, but who are in need of prayer. This board of names just keeps getting bigger and bigger. A lot of people that are on it have no idea that I pray for them.

My desire is not to be great in my own right, but that is what the God of the Universe wants us to understand. We are great. He made us this way. We have had programming from long ago that has kept us from knowing this. I am learning that the more I love myself, the more I love others. I want to lift up others to let them know just how great they are. I want them to know just how much they are loved and just how special they are. I have come to know and experience firsthand how much I am loved, by loving myself. I want them to experience this themselves. I have extreme respect and reverence for God. As I am learning more and more, the greater that I see that I am, the greater He becomes, the more I am aware of everything that I have been given, the more grateful I become, and love just flows from this. We are designed to know ourselves. Everyone can wake up to themselves. You are part of this awakening if you choose to be. You are on this Earth at this very moment to raise the consciousness of it and bring peace to it. We welcome You to You.

Love Is Truth

Aren't You a Christian?

I HAVE BEEN ASKED about going through all these changes as someone with Christian values. I am so grateful for being asked this question, as it has forced me to see what I really know as truth and let go of more in my mind and my heart that no longer serves me. Love is truth. It is freeing just to say this. Our bodies are designed for truth. The scientific name for the study of movement is "kinesi-ology"; my perception of this is that our muscles demon-strate truth from our bodies. I knew that what I had been feeling for the past six months was truth, so I had to do much searching in my heart and researching online to prove to myself that what I was going through was not wrong. I will share some of this with you. I do know that one thing resulting from going through all this for almost two years is a closer relationship to my God and it has changed me for the better. I also see people around me who are in my life and my children's lives who are being affected and changed for the better by all this. They look at their lives with hope, joy, and love. My sons Zachary, Anthony and Cody, and their friends, Brett, Johnny, Austin, Peter, Jose, and Alberto and many others give me hugs every time I see them. This warms my heart. They all know that when they are in my presence they are going to be loved and hugged and I think that is why they spend so much time here. I love them all and they feel, know it, and see it. I am not saying the friends don't feel this in their own homes, because they do. I am just saying that I know they are learning what resonates with them, and it is love. It is incredible to witness. I wish I could name them all, but I don't want to leave any of them out. They know who they are. I love each one of them and they know it. It is magical to know that you are making a difference in young people's lives. They can carry this into the next generation. In fact they need to. "I have given you the message to carry, boys. You know what to do. Change the World."

Why Jesus Came Here

We needed Jesus to come here to show us how much we are loved. He wants us to know this. He didn't come here to just give us rules and regulations. Please don't miss out on this. Give it a chance. He came here because of His extreme love for all of us. He wanted us to get it. He wanted us to wake up. He wants us to understand why he spoke in parables. To me He is asking us, "Do you still not get why I had to come here?" What I see is that He came here to show us that we are love. He is love and you are Him, therefore, you are love.

This is my research and therefore my view of some of what is in the Bible and what it is meant to teach us. Again, I am not saying that it is right or wrong. I am not a scholar and would never claim to be. This is just my research and how I choose to live my life. My friend Marcia is helping me to see that it is my choice. Everything in my life is my choice. She has taught me to say, "I chose to be here, I choose to be here now, I am Love." This is my new programming. Marcia is a complete blessing and gift to me. I found out many things that I did not know when I studied the Bible to become part of the Christian faith. After extensive research of the Bible, which uncovered many perspectives I had not considered previously, my belief is that those who are against seeing that we are love, are the people who are afraid to do anything that may be displeasing to God. Remember that fear comes from the mind, not the heart. I understand this thinking, as this is what I had been taught my whole life. Maybe my research will help some of you.

Some things I found during my research of the Bible and its origins are obvious and some are not so obvious; both are telling. For instance, there are some scriptures in the Bible that are not taken literally by Christians, such as what it says in Matthew 5:30: "And if your right hand causes you to stumble, cut it off and throw it away. It is better for you to lose one part of your body than for your whole body to go into hell." This passage correlates with what it says in Matthew 18:9: "And if your eye causes you to stumble, gouge it out and throw it away. It is better for you to enter life with one eye than to have two eyes and be thrown into the fire of hell." In Luke 14:26 the Bible states, "If anyone comes to me and does not hate father and mother, wife and children, brothers and sisters—yes even their own life—such a person cannot be my disciple." Does this mean that Jesus wanted us to hate our family and ourselves? Did he want us to literally gouge our eyes out? The explanation that I was taught was that this is not what Jesus was saying. He is just trying to show us how important it is to know who He is. Then there are other scriptures that we are to take literally. Does anyone really know for sure what we are and aren't supposed to take literally? Have you cut your hand off? Have you gouged your eye out? I am not perfect and I still have my hands and my eyes. What about you? What I have come to understand through this whole process of my journey is that Jesus came here for us to know ourselves, as we are in essence, Him. Know and love yourself, then you will know and love Him. This is Christ Consciousness that many Christians think is evil. When you have Christ Consciousness, a funny thing happens: you learn that you don't need to do anything except, be. Humbleness comes over you. You finally understand that you are loved, so very loved; and you are special, so special, and we are free. You then realize that everyone else is as well, and you want people to know it! John 8:32 states, "If you hold to my teaching, you are really my disciples. Then you will know the truth and the truth will set you free." God made us in His own image and he wants to set us free with the truth: the truth of knowing your own soul. It wants to be set free.

Were You There? I Wasn't

One thing that I thought about is that anyone who is alive today was not there physically in Biblical times. I know that this is very obvious, but I really needed to break this down to bare bones, so to speak. Nobody that is alive today really knows for sure what happened at that time. We can surmise about what happened and we can also have faith in what the Bible says, but no one really knows for sure that what is written in the Bible is what God really wanted us to live by. Teachings have been passed down for many generations. But where did it all come from? Just like medical doctors have been taught in prestigious colleges to be doctors, their teachings needed to come from somewhere. But from where? From what I understand from the research I did while I was very ill, there was a pretty famous family behind the very first colleges and teachings of medical doctors. The family wanted doctors to sell their products, which were pharmaceutical medications. Products from nature were out of the picture as they couldn't be patented. At that time, it was about money and fear of not being in control. Again, from the mind and not the heart. The same kind of thing could have possibly happened in Jesus' time on Earth, right? Archeologists are finding evidence now about Jesus' life, which some people are dismissing and some people in power are denying. It is up to you to study and learn, and then decide for yourself what you believe.

What Is Really in the Bible?

In my quest to understand more of what the Bible is all about, I found Bart Ehrman, who is a Biblical scholar. He is the author of more than twenty books. He teaches about the Bible, its content and its origin. He teaches that the Gospels actually contradict each other. He says that though each Gospel includes some minor differences in the details, there are other differences that are significant. He says that the book of Luke tells us the disciples never left Jerusalem. They stayed there because for the author of this book, salvation had to come to Jerusalem, which is the capital city of the Jews. Jerusalem is where it is said that Jesus was crucified, resurrected, and ascended to heaven. This is where the disciples saw Him. Mr. Ehrman also says, as I understand him, that in the book of Matthew the author said the disciples did not stay in Jerusalem. This book says that they went up to Galilee. In the book of Matthew, it is Galilee because Galilee is symbolically significant. In the book of Matthew, it is explicit that a person has to keep the Jewish law better than the Scribes or the Pharisees if they are going to enter the kingdom of Heaven. Mr. Ehrman also states that Paul, on the other hand, writes that keeping the Jewish law has nothing to do with salvation. Paul's words tell us that the way a person is right with God, is to believe in the death and resurrection of Jesus. Who is right? Were these authors perhaps writing for different audiences?

Mr. Ehrman also teaches that the Gospels of Matthew, Mark, Luke, and John were not really written by Matthew, Mark, Luke, and John; these books are written anonymously. They are not written in the first person. Most people in the ancient World couldn't read or write, particularly the lower class of people, and they spoke Aramaic. Jesus' followers were members of the lower class. These books are written by highly educated, literate, Greek-speaking Christians from a later decade, who probably weren't followers of Jesus. We don't know who actually wrote them. All we know is that they were probably written outside of Palestine, written in Greek, which was not Jesus' native language or the language of His disciples, and they were probably written 40-50 years after the events they describe. We simply don't know the identity of the authors.

If this is how the Bible was written, who really knows if what it says is what we are to live by? Kind of scary, isn't it? Government was ruling things in that age, also. Does our government lie to us about some things? I think we all know the answer to that question. Don't you think it's possible that those who were in power at that time decided to put into the Bible that which would help them to control the people so that they could stay in power? They were playing on people's fears to make them wary of awakening. This is what I had to decide for myself. I choose not to miss the boat on this one. Jesus' whole point is to love one another. Galatians 5:14 tells us: "For the entire law is fulfilled in keeping this one command: Love your neighbor as yourself." I saw a great T-shirt. You can improvise as you would like but this is what it said: Love thy Neighbor, Thy homeless Neighbor, Thy Muslim Neighbor, Thy black Neighbor, Thy white Neighbor, Thy gay Neighbor, Thy Jewish Neighbor, Thy Christian Neighbor, Thy atheist Neighbor, Thy racist Neighbor, Thy addicted Neighbor. This shirt could go on and on. You can fill in the blanks. I will add "Thy New Age Neighbor."

When Did Separation Become So Important?

Think of it this way. Imagine you were out in the woods one day, and someone shot you. You needed help or you were going to die. Along came a person to help save your life. Would you ask them first what religion they were before they saved your life? Of course you wouldn't. You wouldn't care what religion they believed in. Would you care if the person was a man or woman? Would it matter if the person was Jewish, Muslim, White, Chinese, Black, or Blue? Would it matter if they had lots of money or if they were poor? Would it matter if they were homosexual or heterosexual? Would it matter what country they came from or were born into? No, it wouldn't. None of these things would matter. You would just want their help, right? They are showing their love for you. Love is what matters, not their or your hierarchy, religion, color, sex, sexual preference, or anything else that we use to separate ourselves. When did all this separateness become important? To me it is all political. It is about money and power. Those of us who understand this Christ Consciousness know that they can take our life but we have power over our souls. No one can get to you, unless you let them. We are one.

In my understanding, Constantine decided which books of the Bible went into the Holy Bible. Are you aware that there are many other books that were written that didn't make it into the Bible? There is a Book of Thomas, a Book of Philip, a Book of Mary Magdalene, and many others that never made it into the Bible. Why do you think that is? In the Book of Thomas, I have learned from researching about the Gnostic Christians, they were taught that as you know yourself, you will be known by Him. Jesus taught for seventeen years in India. He knew about the Chakras and everything else that I am being asked to write about. Jesus is trying to get this message to you. Don't be so fearful based on what your mind says and the way you have been living for so long, that you miss it. I am finding out that not everything is what it seems.

If it doesn't look like an orange, smell like an orange, or taste like an orange, it is probably not an orange. What I am trying to say is that if it doesn't feel right, it probably isn't right, and if it does feel right, it probably is right. This is our internal guidance that we have been graciously given. I have been through "both sides" of these paths. I feel, see, know, and have been told many times that "we are one." I feel this in every cell of my being, that we are one with everything that is here. People who have not stepped out of their box are fearful and have not come to this point in their lives, so how can they say this isn't so? How do they know if they haven't been here and experienced what I have experienced and lived what I have lived? There is more to life than what you may have been taught.

In my research I also found that there were several groups of Christians in Biblical times who all thought that they were right. Some had one God, some had two Gods and some had 365 Gods. Most Christians now do not know about the early Gnostic Christians. Gnostic comes from the Greek word "gnosis," which means knowledge. These Gnostic Christians knew they could connect with God by going within themselves. They didn't need Bishops or Priests or Clergy and that scared the heck out of these people who were in power. The people in power wanted to stop these Gnostic Christians, because if this knowledge spread, the leaders would no longer be needed in the positions they held, and the people would have the power to connect with God on their own. These Christians knew and loved themselves and found that they could connect to the Divine on their own. They knew their own soul and the soul is where to find God. They used their intuition. These were Jesus' teachings, which He has been trying to teach the rest of us. They got it. They weren't weird people, they just knew and loved themselves and this connected them with the God inside of them. You may want to read about the texts that were found at Nag Hammadi in Egypt. This may make things a little clearer for you; it helped me immensely.

I am only responsible for myself. These experiences are actually drawing me closer to myself, to Jesus, and to people. It has caused me to forgive and to understand forgiveness. It has caused me to be more loving to people, to do more than just turn the other cheek, to love my enemies, of which I have none, as I love all of humanity. It doesn't matter if they love me back. I love them. I believe that everyone is lost in their own suffering of not knowing who they are. You need to decide if you think that this is what Jesus came to teach us. This change in me has caused me to thank the sun and the moon and the stars. It has caused me to thank the food that I eat and water that I drink and that I use. We are in bondage from our thinking. We are enslaved by our thoughts. Liberate your mind and go out of the box and live from your heart!

All Healing Is Divine

It Is All From the Divine

WE ALL NEED HEALING. All the healing in the World, no matter what conduit is used, whether it is Reiki, Yoga, or the Grotto at Lourdes, France where Mother Mary appeared to St. Bernadette, I believe it is all from God. All the healing that I did to get well, everything that came to me at that time was from my God. I remember saying to Him one day, "Do you want me to just give up and stop fighting to get better?" I remember my dad calling at that time and I told him I just wanted to give up. He said, "No Ang, you can't give up hope. You can't give up. You need to keep fighting." At that time it was a gray day and as I looked out the window in my kitchen, the sun burst through the clouds and there was a rainbow in the sky. That was my answer. That was from my God. The methods of my healing were the "ships" that He sent.

There is a story my dad once told me. There was a man drowning in the water and a ship came by and tried to pull him onto the ship. He replied, "No thanks, it's okay, God is going to rescue me." God then directed a second ship to come by and again a rescue was attempted. Again, the man replied, "No, thanks, God is going to rescue me." A third and final ship came by and again tried to rescue the man drowning in the water. A third and final time the man declined the offer and then he drowned. Sometimes we don't see the answer from God when it is right in front of us the whole time.

Seeing and Understanding

My Eyes Are Opened

I NOW SEE THE TREES, the birds, the flowers, the animals, the ground, the snow, the rain, and the clouds. I now SEE people for who they are and what they are going through. I SEE that everything that God made screams LOVE! I have opened my eyes so that I can SEE clearly. I now SEE clearly that loving God is loving ourselves, so we can love each other and help others feel loved that they may love others. And the Earth will change. You can't help people feel loved by judging them. Judging is also from the mind, from fear of not being good enough. Each of us has our own life to go through and live and it is different for everyone. One of my favorite songs is *Day by Day* written by Sammy Cahn. These lyrics are pure love to me. This song simply states what I have in my heart and why I am here. This is how I try to live, day by day.

You Are the Light

Matthew 5:14 states: "You are light of the World. A city on a hill cannot be hidden. Neither do people light a lamp and put it under a bowl. Instead they put it on its stand, and it gives light to everyone in the house." When you are enlightened by all that is, this is how you will be. This is what Jesus was saying who we truly are. Matthew 5:16 tells us: "In this same way let your light shine before men, that they may see your good deeds and praise your father in Heaven." This awakening is all to bring us closer to God, who is our soul. Don't miss it. This is what Jesus wants us to be, so that we may bring it to this World. He wants us to be loving lights that are happy, joyful, and peaceful. He wants our souls to understand why He came here. God wants us to go inside ourselves, find out who we are, love ourselves, and find Him.

Don't Be Afraid of Stepping out of the Box

I was told by a friend that I was being led down the wrong road, one that she referred to as "new age religion." I was very upset, as I didn't see it that way. The next day, I went out for a walk in my driveway. While walking, I was talking to God, listening to music, listening to the birds sing intermittently, and looking at the sky. I was saying to God, "This can't be wrong, I know what I feel in my heart and in my soul. This is who you are to me. You are the birds and the sky and the trees and snow. You are me and I am one with everything." It was a gray and gloomy day. I looked down to the left hand side of where I was walking and there were two beautiful feathers just lying on the side of the small snow bank. It was as though they were placed there for me to find. The Angels knew that I needed encouragement to get through this challenge and I believe they were letting me know they are always there; and yes, this is all from God. They are His messengers. (This may be hard to understand but the Angels are not separate from us either. It is all part of us.) At the time of finding the two feathers, a strange light shown out of the sky on me and it was raining just on me! It wasn't raining in front of me or in back of me. It was just on me. Almost like a small rain cloud was over my head, but it was different than a raincloud. It was the Angels coming to my aid and enveloping me in love. I could feel it. I walked back down the driveway and there were eight more feathers for me along my path; and yes, I was crying with joy that I was experiencing them this way; as that is what life is. It is experiences.

That night I watched the movie *Frozen*. I had no idea what this movie was about before I watched it. There were many synchronicities in the movie that had also been playing out in my life, but the major one was the song, *Let it Go*. This song was composed by Kristen-Anderson-Lopez and Robert Lopez. The whole song represented me letting go of all the old programming, allowing me to be free. As the character Elsa sang about letting go of the old her, she was able to embrace the new her and use the gift that she had been given. She wasn't backing down and I am not going to, either. The flow that she was releasing from her hands was the type of filigree that I drew all the time, as it represented the flow of God. The kicker of the whole movie was the snowman character, "Olaf." At the end of the movie Elsa had placed a cloud over his head so that he could stay alive no matter what the weather was. This represented the cloud that the Angels put over my head. Incidentally, while watching the movie, Gary had me take a quiz on Facebook about the movie *Frozen* to learn which character I was, and I was "Olaf."

The Raven Feather

The day after experiencing the Angels in my driveway, I was coming to grips with the fact that I was indeed chosen to write this book for the World. I was again walking down my driveway and I was thinking to myself, "Well, maybe I am supposed to do this. Maybe all that I am experiencing is really true." I looked to the ground and saw what appeared to be a large black leaf. There was still some snow so it was very eye-catching against the white background.

I went over to it to pick it up, and found that it was an enormous black feather. I kept hearing "raven." "Look up, raven." I have no idea if this was a raven feather or not, but this is what the guides were telling me it was. I looked up "raven" and this is what I found: "The raven can show us how to go into the dark of our inner self and bring out the light of our true self." Resolving inner conflicts which have long been buried is the deepest power of healing we can possess. The Angels wanted me to let go and teach others to do the same, as this is the deepest power of healing.

The Message

The very next day after I received the raven feather, I was driving with my son, Cody, to meet my husband for breakfast before Cody's basketball game. There are two songs that I listen to constantly as they raise my mood and vibration. They are *Happy* sung by Pharrell Williams and *The Man* sung by Aloe Blacc. In my opinion these songs are complete gifts to the World at this time, as their messages are what the World needs. I recently saw a video on YouTube that presented Pharrell and Oprah talking about his song *Happy*. He was completely overwhelmed with joy, to the point of crying, knowing that people were making many, many videos to his song. They were happy videos. I believe he sensed that this song is bigger than he; just as I have sensed that this message is bigger than I. As we were driving down the road to the basketball game, the song that was playing on the radio was *The Man*. I said to Cody, "Do you know what the Angels are telling me that this song is about?" He said, "No, who?" I said, "I am not sure what Aloe Blacc wrote this song about and I mean no disrespect to him or whoever wrote it, but the Angels are telling me that this song represents us being God. The song represents that we are Him and I am to let everybody know this." We continued to drive down to the end of the road, which took about 10 seconds, and as I stopped at the end of the street a beautiful blue jay feather fell right out of the sky right next to my car door! I opened up my car door, picked it up, and cried. It fell out of thin air. There were no trees, no birds, there was nothing in the sky that we could physically see, from which it could have fallen. We both saw it happen and will remember this beautiful gift forever. The blue jay represents a capacity for fearlessness and vigilance in their tasks, and purity of the soul. God was dancing with me. If you have not heard the song, I will also suggest that you listen to it. The whole song is spiritual and beautiful. I can no longer hide that this is actually happening to me. My guides were telling me, "Don't hide. Face it and tell people." This is what I am here for and what I am being asked to do. Whether people believe or not, is up to them. I am the seed that they are using at the moment to plant these revelations.

We Are to Know and Love Ourselves

We Were Divinely Built

IF YOU WERE TO design something to do a job, you would equip it with everything it needed to do the work, to succeed, to do its job, right? For instance .God made us in His own image. We are fearfully and wonderfully made, right? This is the tip of an iceberg, an extremely general example, as we know that our bodies are intrinsically made to function properly. Here is a brief description of how we are designed: God wanted us to walk, so we have legs, knees and feet; we even have toes so that we are able to balance properly; He wanted us to be able to pick up things and feed ourselves, so we have arms, hands, and fingers; we have eyes to see, ears to hear, a nose to smell, and a mouth to eat and talk, and a brain to use to think and utilize all our senses. Most of these functions are automatic and we don't have to even think about how to use them.

They just work. Our hearts beat continuously, we breathe each breath He gives us, and we don't have to think about how to do this. It happens from the moment we are born. We are equipped with the five senses that everyone recognizes; what if we were equipped with MORE than the five senses? Well, in fact, we are, and some people are scared to go there. Some are not sure how to use the additional senses, and some people just stumble upon it. With all of our physical attributes, God has also given us intuition. If He didn't want us to use this, why would God, who is so loving, give this ability to us? We just aren't programmed to think this way. You don't think that David, while in the fields all those years, used his intuition? You don't think that David meditated while he was outside all the time? How can thinking about nature, God, and life, be considered evil? I have found that there are people who believe this practice to be evil; yet David wrote some of the greatest psalms to God thinking of these blessings while he was outside tending his flock.

Look Between the Lines

There are hundreds of thousands of different species on this Planet. Just think about how many different types of plants there are; how many different types of animals there are; how many different species in the oceans; how many snowflakes fall, none of which is exactly the same. Each blade of grass is different. Why would God not want us to know ourselves? Does it make sense that He wants us to know and discover all of these other blessings, but He doesn't want us to know and love ourselves? We need to look between the lines. There is too much complexity here on Earth for us to ignore the reality of this incredible journey of discovering the Universe and all that is in it, including us.

Let's face it, every religion or lack thereof thinks they are right. Jesus said in Matthew 11:25, "I praise you, Father, Lord of heaven and Earth, because you have hidden these things from the wise and learned, and revealed them to little children." Why do you think that things were hidden from the wise? Have you seen how innocent a little child is? Do little children just have faith that they will be cared for and taken care of? The answer is yes, they do. They have a child-like faith. This is what God wants us to have. Faith in ourselves.

It Is All About You and You Are Worth It

It's You, Yes You

THERE IS MUCH MORE that I could tell you to help you understand that it is only your own fear keeping you from Heaven on Earth. It is a fear that comes from your mind, a fear of facing yourself and of facing the pain of the past. When you live from your heart, you are able to face these fears and let them go. In my opinion, those of us who have come to understand this process of Christ Consciousness, are of love and light, because we have let go of that which no longer serves us; letting go has allowed us to see ourselves and it has allowed us to live from our hearts rather than our minds. It is a continual process. If you want this, too, you must look inside yourself. It takes time, but you are worth it, you have always been worth it, and you always will be worth it.

What I have come to realize through all that I have been taught, heard, and experienced is that this journey in life is about you, for you. Everything in this blessed Universe is there, just for you. Isn't that incredible to think about? The flowers bloom, for you. The stars dance, for you. The rain falls, for you. We need peace on this Planet. To achieve peace, you must discover things that are for you. That serve you. Give to you. It is all about You. It is all within You. This is where the magic is. It is not outside of you and it is not about serving your ego; it is about understanding that you are completely and utterly loved and always have been from the beginning of time. There is no separation.

Gratitude changes everything. Start saying "thank you" out loud for everything. Say good morning to the trees and the flowers that you walk by every day. They are all alive for you. When you step on the grass, understand that each blade of grass is resonating at the 528 Hz love frequency. Grass resonates love! Soak this into your being. Remember that rain and snows are blessed and when they fall to Earth, it is a sacred act of love for you. Everything happens in your life to awaken you. God holds us in his arms and waits patiently for us to awaken to ourselves. It is your choice to do this dance or not. I can tell you that, because of what I have experienced on this journey. I get to awaken to Heaven on Earth every day.

I am grateful that you are reading this book, for you. My two-year journey wasn't easy. You may not need to go through what I did to find out who you are. I really hope you don't; but I am seeing now that it is all blessed. Everything that I went through in my life was to bring me to this point of realization: the realization that it is all about Me for Me and it is all about You for You.

I hope this has helped many people to understand who we truly are. Who *you* truly are. Put your boots on and take the journey. It isn't about effort. It is about surrendering. Let go. Face yourself and wake up. As you do this, you will find that there is always a safe place to land and it is in the arms of, *you.*

And the journey continues ....

I wish you everything in love, light, joy, and peace.
— Namaste

Notes

For additional information, please visit:

Brad Yates—Tapping
http://www.youtube.com/watch?v=heQvpti4uvo

Dr. Emoto
http://www.youtube.com/watch?v=TWAuc9GIvFo

Joshua David Stone, Ph.D.
Soul Psychology Keys to Ascension
http://www.lighttechnology.com/store/catalog/books

Bart Ehrman
http://www.bartdehrman.com/

Wayne Dyer and Tao Te Ching
https://www.youtube.com/watch?v=V4zhQ3M892E

Ravens
http://www.linsdomain.com/totems/pages/raven.htm

Bluejays
http://www.whats-your-sign.com/blue-jay-animal-symbolism.html

Visit the author at:

BlissfulFlow.com
facebook.com/Blissful.Flow
twitter.com/BlissfulFlow111
instagram.com/blissfullyangela

CPSIA information can be obtained at www.ICGtesting.com
Printed in the USA
BVOW07*2102260615

405295BV00001B/1/P